PASSWORDS
to English 1

Michaela Blackledge
Joanna Crewe
Jane Flintoft
Julia Waines

OXFORD
UNIVERSITY PRESS

Great Clarendon Street, Oxford OX2 6DP

Oxford University Press is a department of the University of Oxford. It furthers the University's objective of excellence in research, scholarship, and education by publishing worldwide in

Oxford New York

Auckland Bangkok Buenos Aires Cape Town Chennai Dar es Salaam Delhi Hong Kong Istanbul Karachi Kolkata Kuala Lumpur Madrid Melbourne Mexico City Mumbai Nairobi São Paulo Shanghai Taipei Tokyo Toronto

Oxford is a registered trade mark of Oxford University Press in the UK and in certain other countries

© Michaela Blackledge, Joanna Crewe, Jane Flintoft, Julia Waines

British Library Cataloguing in Publication Data

Data available

ISBN 0 19 832088 4

10 9 8 7 6 5 4 3 2 1

Printed in Italy by Rotolito Lombarda.

Acknowledgements
We are grateful for permission to reproduce the following copyright material:

Stephen Briggs: extract from adaptation of *Johnny and the Dead* by Terry Pratchett (Oxford Playscripts, 2003), copyright © Stephen Briggs 2003, reprinted by permission of Oxford University Press.

Alan Brook: 'Skateboard Damage of £20,000', Bridlington *Free Press* 12.4.01, reprinted by permission of the Editor.

David Calcutt: extract from adaptation of *Dracula* by Bram Stoker (Oxford Playscripts, 2003) copyright © David Calcutt, 1999, reprinted by permission of Oxford University Press.

Roald Dahl: extracts from *Boy - Tales of Childhood* (Cape, 1984), copyright © Roald Dahl 1984, and from 'The Hitch-Hiker' in *The Wonderful World of Henry Sugar and Six More* (Cape, 1977), copyright © Roald Dahl 1977, reprinted by permission of David Higham Associates.

Maria Dixon: review of *Stone Cold* by Robert Swindells from Mrs Mad's Book-a-Rama, www.mrsmad.co.uk, reprinted by permission of the author.

Susan Hitches: recipe for 'Tigger's Malty Flapjacks' from *Pooh's Tasty Smackerels: based on the stories of A A Milne with illustrations by E H Shepard* compiled by Susan Hitches (Hunnypot Library, Methuen Children's Books, an imprint of Egmont Books Ltd, 1997), copyright © 1997 by Michael John Brown, Peter Janson-Smith, Roger Hugh Vaughan, Charles Morgan, and Timothy Michael Robinson, Trustees of the Pooh Properties. Published under licence from The Walt Disney Company and reproduced by permission of Egmont Books Ltd.

Terry Pratchett: extracts from *The Wee Free Men* (Doubleday, 2003), and from *Johnny and the Dead* (Corgi, 1994), reprinted by permission of The Random House Group Ltd.

Noda Rottridge: extract from *Fun Facts: Space* (Harrap, 1990), copyright © Chambers Harrrap Publishers Ltd 1990, reproduced by permission of the publishers.

J K Rowling: extract from *Harry Potter* and the *Philosopher's Stone* (Bloomsbury, 1997), copyright © J K Rowling 1997, reprinted by permission of Christopher Little Literary Agency.

Louis Sachar: *There's A Boy in the Girl's Bathroom* (Bloomsbury, 2001), copyright © Louis Sachar 1987, reprinted by permission of Bloomsbury Publishing Ltd.

Ian Sample: 'What does it take to cut off your own arm?', *The Guardian*, 8 May 2003, copyright © The Guardian 2003, reprinted by permission of Guardian Newspapers Ltd.

E H Shepard: illustration of *Tigger*, copyright under the Berne Convention, colouring copyright © 1970, 1974 by E H Shepard and Egmont Books Ltd, reproduced by permission of Curtis Brown Ltd, London.

Lemony Snicket: extract from *The Bad Beginning: A Series of Unfortunate Events Book 1* (Egmont, 2001), copyright © Lemony Snicket 2001, reproduced by permission of Egmont Books Ltd.

Philip Steele: extract from *The Best Ever Book of Pirates* (Kingfisher, 1997), reprinted by permission of Kingfisher Publications plc.

Advocate Galleries for illustration by Rory Tyger used on Royal Worcester plate

Danbury Mint for advertisement for 'Words of Wisdom' Royal Worcester plate

Exploratorium for 'How to make a lava light' by Eric Muller from 'Salt Volcano' activity in Science Explorer Out and About, copyright © Exploratorium, www.exploratorium.edu

B L Kearley Ltd for illustration by Shirley Tourret 'Death of William Marsh' as used in *The Best Ever Book of Pirates* (Kingfisher, 1997).

Peter Newark's Pictures for facsimile of 'Tryals of Captain John Rackam and Other Pirates' as used in *The Best Ever Book of Pirates* (Kingfisher, 1997).

NSPCC for information 'Surfing Safely: Tips for Young People' from www.nspcc.org.uk

Penguin Books Ltd for front cover of *Stone Cold* by Robert Swindells (Puffin, 1995)

Specs Art for illustration by Richard Berridge of Kidd on gibbet as used in *The Best Ever Book of Pirates* (Kingfisher, 1997).

Usborne Publishing, 83-85 Saffron Hill, London EC1N 8RT, UK for extract from *Where Things Come From: and how they are made* (Usborne Explainers, 1989), copyright © Usborne Publishing Ltd 1989.

Yorkshire Air Museum for information leaflet (2003).

Yorkshire Post Newspapers Ltd for adapted review of 'Pirates of the Caribbean', *The Yorkshire Post*, 8.8.03.

Royal Ontario Museum for explanation of an archaeological dig adapted from 'Pieces of the Past' on www.rom.on.ca

We regret we have been unable to trace and contact all copyright holders of material included before publication. If notified the publisher undertakes to rectify any errors or omissions at the earliest opportunity.

The Publisher would like to thank the following for permission to reproduce photographs:

Corbis Royalty Free: p 50 (left); Jonathan Blair/Corbis: p 32 (left); Arne Hodalic/Corbis: p 32 (right); Charles & Josette Lenars/Corbis: p 6 (right); Corel Professional Photos: pp 19, 20, 36, 88 (left & middle right); Digital Vision: pp 34, 35, 87, 113 (middle); Empics: p 109; Gretel Daugherty/Getty Images: p 21; Carol Ford/Getty Images: p 50 (right); The Image Bank /Getty Images: p 59; Hemera Photo Objects: p 40; Simon Kench/Bridlington Free Press: pp 61, 65 (left); Photodisc: pp 6 (background and centre), 8, 26, 46, 63, 65 (right), 75, 77, 88 (right & middle left), 97, 113 (left & right); Donald Cooper/Photostage: p 90.

Cover photo: Alamy Images

Artwork is by John Adams, Barking Dog, Roger Fereday, Ruth Galloway, Bill Greenhead, Andy Hammond, Grizelda Holdernesse, Sarah Horne, Peter Melnycuk, Matthew Robson and Luke Warm.
Icons by Tim Kahane

The Best Ever Book of Pirates by Philip Steele: pp 10 & 11. Artwork is by Richard Berridge/Specs Art

Tiggers Malty Flapjacks from Pooh's Tasty Smackerels/Hunnypot Library: p 39. Illustration copyright © Ernest H Shepard & Methuen Children's Books Ltd.

The authors and publisher would like to thank the many teachers, advisers, and schools who assisted in the research and trialling of *Passwords to English*.

Contents

Introduction   4

Unit 1   Information texts   5

Unit 2   Recounts   18

Unit 3   Explanations   28

Unit 4   Instructions   38

Unit 5   Persuasive texts   48

Unit 6   Discursive texts   58

Unit 7   Advice texts   70

Unit 8   Description   80

Unit 9   Plays   90

Unit 10   Poetry   104

Unit 11   Stories   115

Unit 12   Reviews and reading journals   131

Quiz: Features of text types   141

Introduction

Welcome to *Passwords to English*!

Passwords can open up exciting new places. This book will take you into the world of English. You will read about a man who cut off his own arm, a boy who talks to ghosts, two evil Counts, how to make your own volcano, the arguments for and against skateboarding, and get to write about the things that interest *you*!

Look for these symbols to help you:

 This means there's a text for you to read.

 This means there's a starter activity to do.

Password	Audience
	The **audience** is the people who read the text.

Key things you need to know and understand are explained.

 This section helps you to remember what you have learnt.

 This means it is your turn to think about your own text.

 This means to start writing!

→ Remember!

Persuasive texts may use:
➤ repetition
➤ exaggeration
➤ rhetorical questions
➤ imperatives.

Use the Remember panels to remind yourself of the main points in each unit. At the back of the book is a quiz that you can use with a partner!

There's lots to do in this book, as well as lots to read, talk and write about. So turn the pages and enjoy it!

Michaela Blackledge
Joanna Crewe
Jane Flintoft
Julia Waines

In this unit you will:

➤ explore the features of information texts
➤ write an information text.

Get started

Information texts are all around us. They are part of our daily lives. They are on food packaging, in the streets, on posters, in magazines, in books, on the computer. So, what exactly are information texts?

They come in different forms, but they all give us knowledge – facts and details.

With a partner, think about all the places that you find information texts during the day. Start from first thing in the morning and work through your day. List your ideas.

1. breakfast cereal packet
2. toothpaste box
3.
4.
5.

Information about space

Read this information text.

Comets and Meteors

Heads and tails

Comets are balls of dust and ice particles which travel in an oval-shaped orbit around the Sun. They glow because they reflect the Sun's light.

A comet has a head and a tail, a trail of gas and dust. The longest comet tails measure hundreds of millions of kilometres.

Some astronomers have suggested that life may have first reached Earth when a comet crashed on the surface.

Space rocks

Meteors are small pieces of rock or dust left behind by a comet. When they enter the Earth's atmosphere they usually burn up, producing brief streaks of light known as shooting stars.

Some of the biggest meteors get through the atmosphere and land on Earth. They are called meteorites.

Asteroid origins

Meteorites may be rocks which have broken off from asteroids, larger lumps of rock orbiting the Sun between the inner planets and the outer planets of the Solar System. The largest asteroid, called Ceres, is as big as France!

Look out!

When meteorites land, they create holes called craters in the ground. Some craters are very large; one famous crater in Arizona measures 1 km across and 175 m deep!

Meteorites have been known to cause damage, such as tree destruction, but this is very rare.

Text from *Space* by Noda Rottridge

What people do you think are the **audience** for this information text?

Password →	**Audience**
	The **audience** is the people who read the text.

 What clues helped you to decide on the audience?

3 Look at the verbs in this information text. What **tense** are they written in?

Password →	**Tense**
	Verbs can be written in the **past**, **present** or **future tense**.
	For example:
	The meteor *crashed* into Earth. (past tense)
	The meteor *crashes* into Earth. (present tense)
	The meteor *will crash* into Earth. (future tense)

4 Rewrite these sentences, changing the verbs into the present tense.

➤ The planet Mars *had* two moons.
➤ Earth *will be* part of the Solar System.
➤ Nine planets *travelled* around the Sun.
➤ When meteorites land, they *will create* holes in the ground.

5 Read this sentence:

'Meteors are small pieces of rock or dust left behind by comets.'

What **person** is it written in? Is it first, second or third person?

Password →

Person

Text can be written in different forms of **person**.

For example:
  I am taking down the landing pod. (first person – uses 'I' or 'we')
  You are driving the space buggy. (second person – uses 'you')
  Moons circle planets. (third person – uses 'he', 'she', 'it', 'they')

The third person form is impersonal. It is often used to give information.

6 Read these sentences. Are they written in the first, second or third person form?

➤ The Sun is a star.
➤ You must wear a gum shield when you play rugby.
➤ He sat on his only pair of sunglasses.
➤ I'll pick you up outside the cinema.
➤ They thought snow-boarding looked fun.
➤ I chose a bad time to speak to the Head teacher.

7 Scan the information text again. Select five facts about comets. Copy and complete the list below.

Facts
1. a comet has a head and a tail, a trail of gas and dust.
2.
3.
4.
5.

8 The author divides up the information on the page into sections. How do we know what each section is about?

9 Can you think of other sub-headings that could be used for these sections?

10 Look at the different types of sentences in the text.

➤ Write down two short, simple sentences.
➤ Write down two longer, **complex sentences**.

Why do you think the writer uses a mix of sentence types?

Password ➜

Complex sentences

A **complex sentence** has a *main clause* and at least one *subordinate clause*.

➤ A *main clause* makes sense on its own. It can form a sentence.
➤ A *subordinate clause* does not make sense on its own. It depends on the main clause.

For example:

Main clause

The largest asteroid, called Ceres, is as big as France!

Subordinate clause

11 Copy out these sentences and underline the subordinate clauses.

➤ After finishing his pudding, Josh had a bar of chocolate.
➤ Alex spent hours tidying her room, something she hated.

Information about pirates

Read the text below. It is from a book about pirates.

A pirate's death

Few pirates lived to enjoy their wealth. Some, like the English corsair Sir Henry Mainwaring, gained a royal pardon and abandoned piracy. Most pirates died in distant lands, in brutal battles. Thomas Tew was shot during an attack on the Mogul ship *Fateh Muhammad* in 1695. Thomas Anstis was killed in the Caribbean in about 1723, murdered by his own crew. John Ward, who turned Barbary corsair under the name 'Yusuf Raïs', died of plague in Tunis in 1622. The ones who made it home, like Henry Avery, often died penniless and forgotten.

Death of William Marsh

William de Marisco, or Marsh, was a pirate based on the island of Lundy, in the Bristol Channel. He was captured in 1242 and taken to London. There he was hauled through the streets, hanged, quartered (chopped into four pieces) and burned.

► Large crowds turned out to watch pirates being hanged at Execution Dock by the River Thames. Their bodies were placed in iron cages so that no one could steal the bones and bury them.

THE
TRYALS
OF
Captain John Rackam,
AND OTHER
PIRATES, *Viz.*

Geroge Fetherston,   Noah Harwood,
Richard Corner,   James Dobbins,
John Davies,   Patrick Carty,
John Howell,   Thomas Earl,
Tho. Bourn, *alias* Brown, John Fenwick, *al'* Fenis

Who were all Condemn'd for PIRACY, *at the Town of St. Jago de
la Vega, in the Island of* JAMAICA, *on Wednesday and Thursday
the Sixteenth and Seventeenth Days of November 1720.*

AS ALSO, THE
TRYALS *of* Mary Read *and* Anne Bonny,
alias Bonn, *on Monday the 28th Day of the
said Month of* November, *at St. Jago
de la Vega aforesaid.*

And of several Others, who were also condemn'd for PIRACY.

ALSO,

A True Copy of the Act of Parliament made for the more effectual suppression of Piracy.

Jamaica: Printed by Robert Baldwin, in the Year 1721.

▲ Everyone wanted to read reports of the trial of John Rackham (Calico Jack), Anne Bonny and Mary Read. In the 1700s, popular songs were written about such pirates and their evil deeds.

From earliest times, laws against piracy were savage. Captured pirates were tortured and enslaved. The Romans nailed pirates to crosses. The German pirate Stortebeker had his head cut off in Hamburg in 1402. English pirates of the 1700s were hanged at Execution Dock in London. The tide was allowed to wash over their bodies, which were then tarred and hung in chains as a warning to all – piracy never pays.

From *The Best-Ever Book of Pirates* by Philip Steele

1 In many information texts, paragraphs start with a **topic sentence**. Write a different topic sentence for the first paragraph of the text you have just read.

Password →

Topic sentences

A **topic sentence** tells the reader what the paragraph is about. It is usually at the beginning of a paragraph.

For example:
'There are strict rules in a football game, which players must follow.'

This could be a topic sentence at the beginning of a paragraph about the rules of football.

2 Pick out two more topic sentences in this extract.

3 Information texts need to be organized clearly, so the reader can find the information they need easily. They are often laid out in sections with headings, sub-headings, captions and pictures.

Compare the layout of the two texts you have read. Use the grid below to help you. Write examples of the features you find.

Layout features	Comets and Meteors	A Pirate's Death
Headings	Heads and tails	Death of William Marsh
Text broken up into sections	Four sections	
Pictures		
Captions		
Specialist words		
Different font sizes, colours and shapes		
Facts and figures, e.g. times, dates, names		

An information leaflet

Read this information leaflet.

YORKSHIRE AIR MUSEUM

- ALLIED AIR FORCES MEMORIAL
- AUTHENTIC WWII BOMBER BASE
- OVER 40 HISTORIC AIRCRAFT

YORKSHIRE AIR MUSEUM
ELVINGTON · YORK

HOW TO FIND US

Scarborough
Malton
Bridlington
York
Leeds
A64 Bypass
A1079
B1228
Sutton on Derwent
Howden
Pocklington
Elvington
Hull
AIR MUSEUM

From the York by-pass, take the Hull exit (A1079) and then immediate right to Elvington (B1228), the Museum is sign-posted on the right.

OPENING HOURS

We are open every day, 10.00am to 5.00pm, (In winter, 10.00am to 3.30pm)
Closed Christmas Day and Boxing Day

FACILITIES & FREE P

YORK TOURISM AWARDS 2000 WINNER

YORKSHIRE TOURIST BOARD White Rose Awards for Tourism 2001 WINNER

WHY NOT JOIN US?

Support the Museum - Join Now and receive regular magazines
Annual Membership £15.00

FULL NAME IN BLOCK CAPITALS
....

ADDRESS ....
..............................POST CODE ....

Please send cheques payable to:
Yorkshire Air Museum, Halifax Way, Elvington, York, YO41 4AU or hand in at the Stewards Office.

Please tick here for:
☐ Standing Order Form
☐ Info on being a Volunteer
☐ Deed of Covenant Form (to reclaim tax)

For further information please contact:-
YORKSHIRE AIR MUSEUM
Halifax Way, Elvington, York YO41 4AU
(01904) 608595. Fax: (01904) 608246
www.yorkshireairmuseum.co.uk

YORKSHIRE AIR MUSEUM Canada Branch
(Doug Sample, CD)
470 Petit Street, St Laurent
(Quebec) Canada, H4N 2H6
(514) 744 6309 · Fax: (514) 744 1395

REGISTERED MUSEUM

Registered Charity No. 56766

13

2003 MAIN EVENTS

4/5	May	Battlegroup North
16	May	Dambusters 60th Anniversary
8	June	100 Years of Flight
12	June	Womens Air Memorial Day
22	June	Airborne Show
3	July	Air Gunners Day
5	July	Lecture Symposium
6	July	Cayley Day – Centuries of Flight
10	Aug	The York Classic and Superbike Rally
7	Sept.	RAFA Battle of Britain Day

Famous WWII adversaries discuss tactics at one of our reunion days

Our unique WWII Halifax Bomber

Events, displays and re-enactments throughout the year

Lots of fun for young and old alike

Phil Harding from Channel 4's Time Team – Schools Millennium Challenge

YORKSHIRE AIR MUSEUM

Occupying the operational site of the former RAF Elvington the Yorkshire Air Museum is the largest WWII Bomber Command Station open to the public in the country.

From the base, British, Canadian and French aircrews flew on missions to Europe. The airfield is typical of the many that were spread around the whole area filling the skies with the sound of heavy bombers night after night. It is now a living memorial to the allied air forces who served in Yorkshire during the war. In addition to the numerous exhibits tracing the history of aviation, the museum is renowned for its unique atmosphere and its many special events throughout the year.

- Authentic buildings housing displays and exhibitions incorporating the Airborne Forces, RAF Regiment, Archives, Barnes Wallis Collection and much more.
- Restored Control Tower featuring the sounds of a WWII Bomber Station.
- The Air Gunners Room pays tribute to the bravery of the gunner in his turret.
- Squadron Memorial Rooms and Gardens that includes the unique memorial to the Women's Air Service.
- The only historic aircraft collection to feature authentic replicas of the Cayley Glider and Wright Flyer alongside WWII aircraft and modern jets.
- Gifts and Souvenirs available from our Museum Shop.
- Uniquely atmospheric Conference and Corporate Event facilities in the various exhibition halls and buildings.

Come and share the experience in this Centenary Year of Aviation History!

1 Imagine you are going to visit the Air Museum. Use the information on this leaflet to answer these questions:

➤ Where is it?
➤ When is it open?
➤ What are some of the main events?
➤ How can I contact the museum?

2 Who do you think is the **audience** for this information text? Give reasons for your answer, using examples from the leaflet.

3 What **tense** is this information text written in? Explain why this tense is appropriate, to a partner.

4 Which of the following layout features are used in this leaflet?

a) bullets
b) headings and sub-headings
c) graphs
d) colour
e) photographs
f) illustration
g) captions

Round-up

You have looked at three information texts. With a partner, list six features that are important in an information text.

Over to you

You now know enough about information texts to have a go at writing your own. Chose one of the topics below:

➤ your school
➤ your family
➤ your pet
➤ your favourite sport
➤ a subject of your own choice.

> → **Remember!**
>
> Information texts use:
> ➤ the present tense
> ➤ the third person
> ➤ clear layout (sub-headings, topic sentences, illustration)
> ➤ They are written for a particular audience.

Plan

Begin by jotting down ideas in a mind map, like the one below.

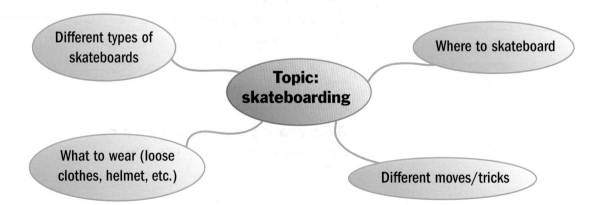

Now plan out your paragraphs in boxes. Each paragraph should contain a section of text. Write a topic sentence at the top of each box, then the notes for the paragraph below.

> **There are lots of different types of skateboards.**
>
> Special ones for 'tricks'
> Cheap ones for beginners
> Ones to build yourself...

> **Some skateboarding moves are easy, but others need a lot of practice.**
>
>

> **It is important to wear the right kit, for comfort, movement and safety.**
>
> Helmet
> Knee & elbow pads
> Baggy clothes so you can bend
> No bits hanging near wheels

> **Skateboard parks are common but many people prefer to use the streets.**
>
>

Now write your information text in full.

In this unit you will:

➤ look at different recount texts and identify how they are written
➤ write a personal recount using a variety of sentence structures.

How will I recount this to my friends?

Get started

A recount retells events. When you tell your friends what you have been doing, you are giving a recount. In pairs or small groups, tell each other what you did last night or at the weekend, or in the holidays.

Recounts are often written down. Here are some examples of written recounts: a postcard, a newspaper story, an autobiography, a biography.

A postcard

Read this postcard.

Dear Poppy,

Yesterday, I arrived in busy but beautiful Paris. Hasn't been much of a rest as I've visited so many places.

First, I went to the Eiffel Tower, which was very impressive but I didn't have time to go to the top. Next, I jumped on a tour bus which stopped at the Notre Dame cathedral, the Louvre art gallery and the Arc de Triomphe. Was glad I wasn't driving as the French seemed a bit crazy on the roads!

Later, I stopped in a lovely street café for some lunch and then I visited the Pompidou Centre. Finally, I relaxed on a gentle cruise along the River Seine – a lovely ending to a pretty manic day.

Love Amy xxx

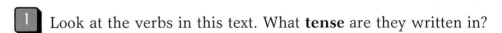

1 Look at the verbs in this text. What **tense** are they written in?

Password →

Tense

Verbs can be written in the **past, present** or **future tense**.

For example:
 I *climbed* the tower. (past tense)
 I *climb* the tower. (present tense)
 I *will climb* the tower. (future tense)

2 Most recounts are written in the past tense. Why?

3 With a partner, decide which of the sentences below are written in the past tense.

➤ We went to the pool.
➤ We will be going on an aeroplane.
➤ The weather is stormy.
➤ I posted the letter yesterday.
➤ Jack lost his football boots.

4 Change the other sentences into the past tense.

5 Most recounts are written in **chronological order**. Does Amy write her recount in chronological order? How can you tell?

Password →

Chronological order

Chronological order means the order in which things happen.

For example, if you wrote about a trip to Alton Towers, you might write about when you arrived, then your first ride, then your second ride, etc.

6 You can show chronological order with a time line. Copy and complete the time line below. It shows the chronological order of Amy's day. Use the postcard to help you.

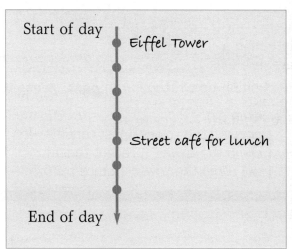

Start of day
 Eiffel Tower

Street café for lunch

End of day

7 Recounts often use **connectives** to show the sequence of events. List the time connectives in the postcard.

Password →

Connectives

Connectives link clauses or sentences. Recounts often use time connectives, e.g. *first, next, then, later*.

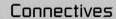

A newspaper story

Read this newspaper story.

What does it take to cut off your own arm?

More than dedication, that's for sure, as Aron Ralston found out last week. Ralston, from Aspen, Colorado, was climbing alone in a remote canyon 241 km south-east of Salt Lake City when he dislodged a 350 kg boulder that fell on his right forearm, pinning it, and so him, against the rock face.

After three days and no sign of rescue, his water ran out. Two days later, Ralston figured it was decision time: lose the limb or lose his life. He pulled a tourniquet tight around his right bicep, got out a small penknife and set about hacking through his forearm. Having cut his arm back to a stump, he used ropes to lower himself 25 metres to the bottom of the canyon where he set about finding help.

'People can do superhuman things under pressure, but this is different,' says Simon Lambert, an upper limb surgeon at the Royal National Orthopaedic Hospital in Stanmore. 'This is a conscious decision – I'm going to cut my arm off. It's not about a superhuman physical effort, this was an extraordinarily mentally strong man.'

Because he was climbing, Ralston may not have felt the full brunt of the pain when the boulder first landed on him. When you are doing something dangerous, natural endorphins start rushing around your blood stream, ready to act as painkillers should the worst happen. But they would only have been effective for a few hours. By then, most of the crushed limb would have gone numb for good. 'After an hour and a half of a 350 kg boulder lying on your arm, the nerves and muscle tissue below the crush line will be dead,' says Lambert. 'The boulder would have done the major part of the amputation itself.'

Article by Ian Sample, *The Guardian*, 8 May 2003

21

1 The grid below lists key features of recounts. Copy and complete the grid to find out whether most of the newspaper article is a recount. Give examples of the features you find.

Recounts	Yes	No
Written in the past tense		
Written in chronological order		
Uses time connectives		

2 Some recounts use short simple sentences. Others use longer, **complex sentences**. What sort of sentences does this newspaper story use?

Password →

Complex sentences

A **complex sentence** has a *main clause* and at least one *subordinate clause*.

➤ A *main clause* makes sense on its own. It can form a sentence.
➤ A *subordinate clause* does not make sense on its own. It depends on the main clause.

For example:

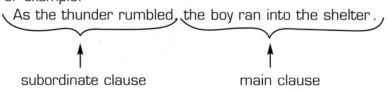

    As the thunder rumbled, the boy ran into the shelter.

       subordinate clause   main clause

3 Why do you think newspaper recounts often use complex sentences? (Think about how much information you can get in a complex sentence, compared to a simple one.)

4 Copy out the following sentences and underline the subordinate clauses. (Remember, they don't always come at the start of a sentence.)

➤ Although I felt a bit sick, I had another go on the ride.
➤ I watched the film even though it was a bit boring.
➤ Whilst eating a large cream cake, Grandma smiled at me.
➤ Paul, who had just left hospital, was glad to be home.

> When you write complex sentences, remember to vary the structure of them. This will make your writing more interesting.

5 In the newspaper story, direct speech adds a personal comment and confirms what the journalist has written. Look at how the direct speech is punctuated:

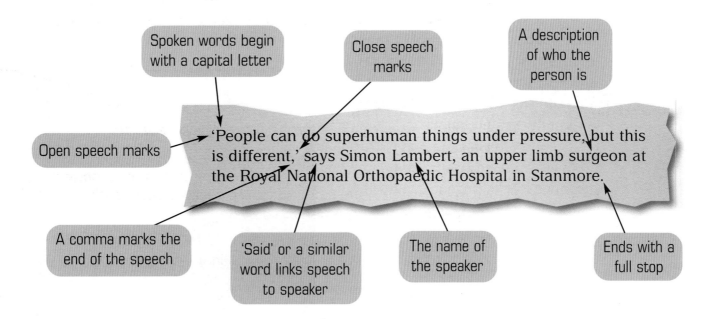

Spoken words begin with a capital letter

Close speech marks

A description of who the person is

Open speech marks

'People can do superhuman things under pressure, but this is different,' says Simon Lambert, an upper limb surgeon at the Royal National Orthopaedic Hospital in Stanmore.

A comma marks the end of the speech

'Said' or a similar word links speech to speaker

The name of the speaker

Ends with a full stop

6 Rewrite the following sentence and add the correct punctuation, including speech marks.

A fantastic goal shouted the commentator. That boy can certainly put them in the back of the net.

An autobiography

Here is another recount. It is from Roald Dahl's autobiography, *Boy – Tales of Childhood*, where the author describes a visit to the doctor. As in many recounts, this includes description as well as action.

The doctor was bending over me. In his hand he held that long shiny steel instrument. He held it right in front of my face, and to this day I can still describe it perfectly. It was about the thickness and length of a pencil, and like most pencils it had a lot of sides to it. Toward the end, the metal became much thinner, and at the very end of the thin bit of metal there was a tiny blade set at an angle. The blade wasn't more than a centimetre long, very small, very sharp and very shiny.

'Open your mouth,' the doctor said, speaking Norwegian.

I refused. I thought he was going to do something to my teeth, and everything anyone had ever done to my teeth had been painful.

'It won't take two seconds,' the doctor said. He spoke gently, and I was seduced by his voice. Like an ass, I opened my mouth.

The tiny blade flashed in the bright light and disappeared into my mouth. It went high up into the roof of my mouth, and the hand that held the blade gave four or five very quick little twists and the next moment, out of my mouth into the basin came tumbling a whole mass of flesh and blood.

I was too shocked and outraged to do anything but yelp. I was horrified by the huge red lumps that had fallen out of my mouth into the white basin and my first thought was that the doctor had cut out the whole of the middle of my head.

'Those were your adenoids,' I heard the doctor saying.

I sat there gasping.

1 Prove that this is a recount:

- ➤ find three verbs in the past tense
- ➤ find three events written in chronological order.

2 Roald Dahl has used many adjectives to create a powerful description of his visit to the doctor. Copy and complete the following table by finding four more adjectives and nouns. (Remember, an adjective describes a noun.)

Adjective	Noun
tiny	blade

3 The writer has also used some powerful verbs to describe how he felt. Find two.

4 Roald Dahl has written some very short sentences, e.g. 'I refused.' and 'I sat there gasping.' Why do you think he has done this?

Round-up

With a partner, decide on three main features of recounts.
Think carefully about the texts you have looked at.
Check that they use some of the features you have chosen.

Over to you

Have a go at writing your own personal recount. Here are some suggestions for topics:

➤ a memorable day out
➤ an accident
➤ a visit to the dentist/hospital
➤ a great present
➤ an important family occasion.

When you write a personal recount (something that actually happened to you), remember to use the first person, 'I ...'.

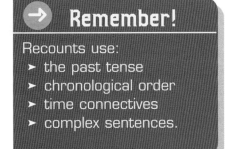

→ Remember!

Recounts use:
➤ the past tense
➤ chronological order
➤ time connectives
➤ complex sentences.

Plans

Use a time line to plan your recount (see page 20). Or, cut out some pieces of scrap paper and on each one write an idea for a paragraph. Put them in chronological order. Remember to include some direct speech – but not too much!

Here is an outline plan and an example of one filled in. A few sketches may help your planning.

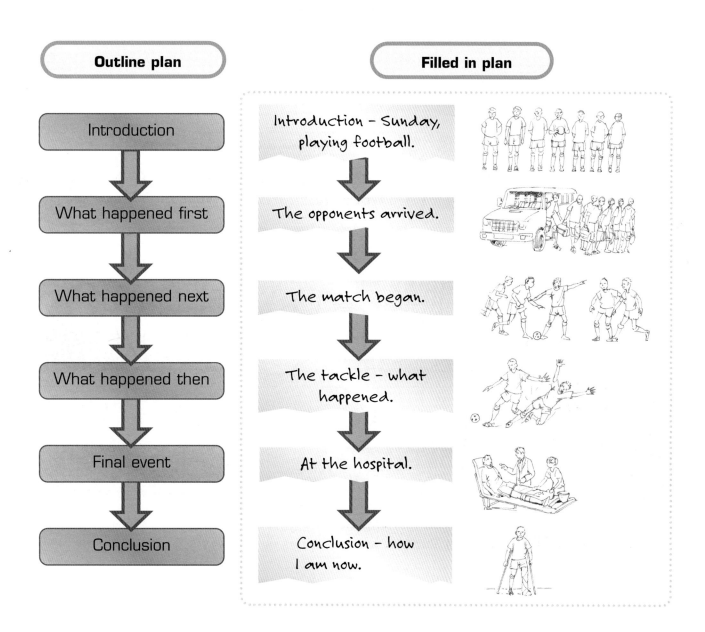

Outline plan

- Introduction
- What happened first
- What happened next
- What happened then
- Final event
- Conclusion

Filled in plan

- Introduction – Sunday, playing football.
- The opponents arrived.
- The match began.
- The tackle – what happened.
- At the hospital.
- Conclusion – how I am now.

Use your plan to write your recount.

Explanations

In this unit you will:

➤ look at how explanations are written and laid out
➤ write an explanation of your own.

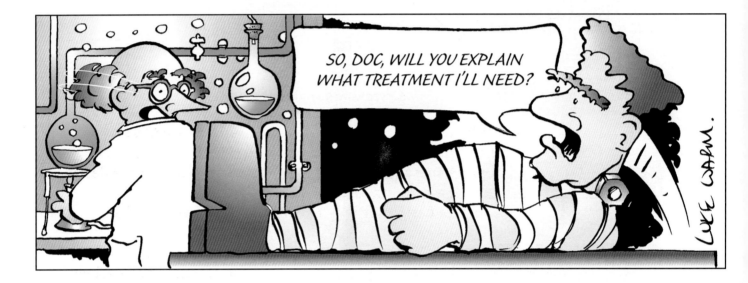

Get started

Explanations often answer questions. They help you to understand things, such as what happens or the way something works.

You will have heard or given explanations in many lessons. For example:

➤ Maths – how to solve a problem using estimating or a calculator
➤ Science – why animals hibernate
➤ History – why a country went to war
➤ Geography – how global warming affects the planet.

Test how good you are at giving explanations!

➤ Draw a simple design (without letting anyone else see it). You could use one of these designs:

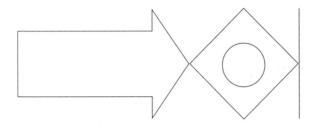 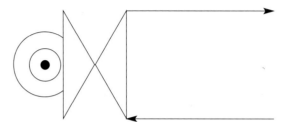

➤ Explain your design, carefully and clearly, to a partner or the rest of the group.
➤ Your partner (or the rest of the group) has to draw your design, following your explanation.
➤ Compare designs. If they match, you have given a good explanation!
➤ If they don't match, perhaps you didn't explain things in a sensible order, or give clear details – or perhaps your audience wasn't listening carefully!

Explaining a process

Read the explanation on the next page about 'How chocolate is made'.

 This explanation is to:

a) help you make chocolate
b) help you understand how chocolate is made
c) help you decide whether you like the taste of chocolate.

(Choose the right answer.)

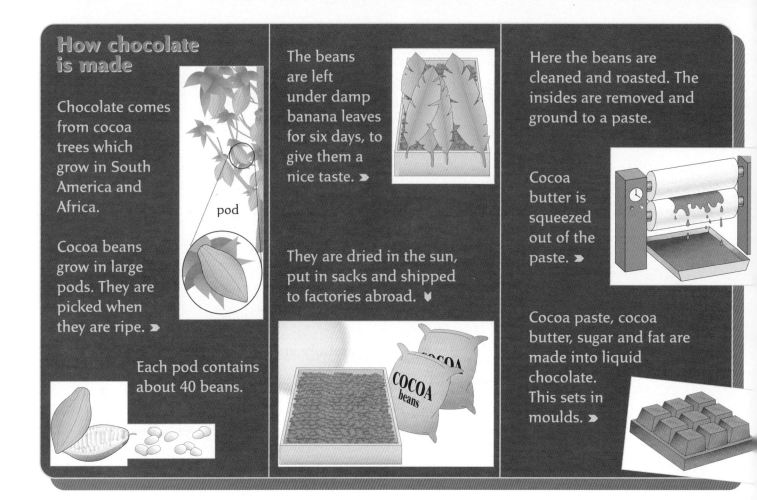

How chocolate is made

Chocolate comes from cocoa trees which grow in South America and Africa.

Cocoa beans grow in large pods. They are picked when they are ripe. ➤

Each pod contains about 40 beans.

pod

The beans are left under damp banana leaves for six days, to give them a nice taste. ➤

They are dried in the sun, put in sacks and shipped to factories abroad. ⬇

COCOA beans

Here the beans are cleaned and roasted. The insides are removed and ground to a paste.

Cocoa butter is squeezed out of the paste. ➤

Cocoa paste, cocoa butter, sugar and fat are made into liquid chocolate. This sets in moulds. ➤

2 Which **tense** is the explanation written in?

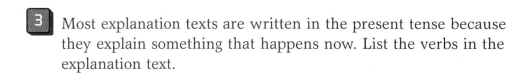

Tense

Verbs can be written in the **past**, **present** or **future tense**.

For example:
> The cocoa beans *were picked*. (past tense)
> The cocoa beans *are picked*. (present tense)
> The cocoa beans *will be picked*. (future tense)

3 Most explanation texts are written in the present tense because they explain something that happens now. List the verbs in the explanation text.

4 Look at the illustrations. Why do you think they are included?

5 Why are there arrows next to the illustrations?

6 Who is the audience for this explanation? (Remember, the audience is the people who read the text.) How can you tell?

7 Look again at the text. The explanation is written using the third **person** form. Why is this useful for explanation texts?

Password →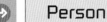

Person

Text can be written in different forms of **person**.

For example:
I picked the cocoa beans. (first person)
You picked the cocoa beans. (second person)
The cocoa beans were picked. (third person)

The third person form is impersonal and is often used to give factual information.

8 How does the writer **sequence** the text? (Think about the order of the sentences.)

Password →

Sequence

The **sequence** is the order in which something is done or laid out, so that it works or makes sense.

For example, to have a drink, you need to go to the fridge, open the door, take out the can, open it, then drink. You cannot drink without doing all the things before in the right order!

9 Look back at the text about making chocolate. Would it still make sense if the sequence of sentences was different?
(Hint: test this with a partner by reading out the sentences in random order. Does the explanation still make sense?)

Explaining an activity

 The following text looks different from the last one on page 30. Is it an explanation? Work with a partner to decide on your answer. Look for the key features of explanations:

➤ present tense
➤ third person
➤ a clear sequence.

Just as you need a licence to drive a car, archaeologists have to get a licence *before* they can dig (or **excavate**) a site. Each licence is good for one site and one year. When she gets a licence, an archaeologist agrees to write a site report, telling the world what she finds.

Once the archaeologist has received the licence, she is ready to **survey** the site. Surveying is like taking a huge piece of graph paper and placing it down over the site. The graph is called a **site grid**.

The next step is to remove the grass and topsoil. Grass is removed with shovels by digging up the soil in narrow and shallow strips. Then the topsoil is removed by skimming the surface with the shovel blade, taking a thin layer of soil off the surface.

Now the excavation is ready to begin. Sites are usually dug in square **units**. Special attention is paid to **layers** and **features**. Believe it or not, the ground is arranged in layers, like a kind of cake. You can tell when you've reached a new layer when the colour of the soil, or its make-up (texture) changes. A feature is an artefact that is too large to move. A feature might be anything from a filled-in pit to a foundation wall or floor.

Dirt is **sifted** through a screen to make sure no artefacts were missed while digging. Artefacts found in each layer are bagged separately from the ones found in the layer(s) above and below it. Detailed notes, photos, and maybe even videos are taken about everything that is done or found on the site while digging.

Adapted from Pieces of the Past *www.rom.on.ca*

2 What would be a suitable title for this text? (Think about the main topic.)

3 What is the purpose of this text?

a) to explain how to become an archaeologist
b) to explain what sort of things archaeologists find
c) to explain how an archaeological dig is organized.

(Choose the correct answer.)

4 Each **paragraph** focuses on one aspect of the dig. Read each paragraph again and write a summary of what is covered in that paragraph. The first one has been done for you.

Paragraph	Summary
1	getting a licence to start a dig
2	
3	
4	
5	

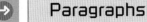

Password →

Paragraphs

A **paragraph** is a section of text. Writers start a new paragraph to show there is a new topic or a different viewpoint.

The first sentence in a paragraph often tells us what the paragraph is about. It is called a *topic sentence*.

5 Look back at the text. It includes some **technical language**, such as:

➤ excavate
➤ features
➤ sifted.

Explain the meaning of these terms in your own words. You may need to use a dictionary.

Password →

Technical language

Words that are used in a special way with a particular subject are called **technical language**.

For example:
In Technology you may use a *router* to shape wood. In Science you use a *test tube* to carry out an *experiment*.

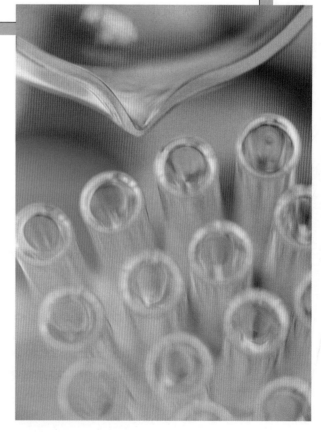

6 Write three sentences about archaeology, using technical language from the extract. You could use the words you explained in Activity 5, or you could choose others.

7 Read the sentences below and select the technical words.

➤ Water trapped by a dam passes through turbines to make electricity.
➤ Early Viking ships had a prow at both ends.
➤ If your circuit stops working, you should check the fuse first.

8 With a partner, discuss why you chose the words that you did. Then, list examples of technical language that you use in other subjects. For example:

➤ Geography – *climate, urban*
➤ Maths – *angle, volume*
➤ ICT – *modem, icon*

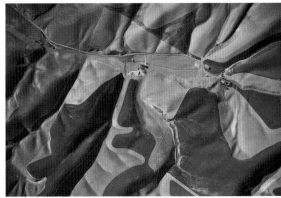

Round-up

Think about what you have learnt about explanations. With a partner, decide on four important features of explanation texts.

Over to you

Now it's your turn to write an explanation. Here are some suggested titles:

➤ What happens when a volcano erupts
➤ How a festival is celebrated
➤ How seeds grow into plants.

Write your explanation for young children. You will need to keep your sentences short and your words easy to understand.

Remember!

Explanations use:
- ➤ the present tense
- ➤ the third person
- ➤ sequence (to link points clearly)
- ➤ clear paragraphs
- ➤ technical language.

Plan

Plan out your ideas before you start writing. Remember to think about your audience (readers). Follow these steps:

1. Think of a title for your explanation.

2. Write down your main idea for each paragraph.

3. Put your paragraphs into a clear sequence.

4. Think about technical language that you want to use.

5. Think about pictures that you want to use.

6. Check you have used the present tense and the impersonal third person form.

Now write your explanation in full.

In this unit you will:

➤ identify and use imperative verbs
➤ look at how instructions are clearly sequenced
➤ write instructions that are easy to follow.

'Brake pads? Oooops! I should have followed the instructions!'

KIT CAR

BRAKE PADS

Get started

Instructions can be important. They can tell you what to do in an emergency, or how to get somewhere, or how to make something. Instructions take the reader through a process, step by step. You can find instructions in many different places, such as in cookery books (recipes), in leaflets (e.g. setting up a new DVD player), on signs (e.g. fire escape instructions), and in games.

With a partner, list instructions that you have come across recently. They might be at home, at school or in town.

Recipe

Read this recipe.

Tigger's malty flapjacks

Kanga said, "oh!" and then clutched at the spoon again just as it was disappearing, and pulled it safely back out of Tigger's mouth. But the Extract of Malt had gone.

Ingredients:
50g (4oz) butter or margarine
3 tablespoons of syrup
2 tablespoons malt
250g (8oz) porridge oats

You will need:
Large saucepan
Wooden spoon
Tablespoon
20cm (8in.) baking tin

Set the oven to 190°F, Gas Mark 5

 **1.** Grease the baking tin.

 2. Melt the butter, syrup and malt gently in a saucepan over a low heat until melted.

 3. Take the pan off the heat and stir in the porridge oats.

 4. Spread out in the baking tin and press down firmly with the back of the spoon.

 **5.** Bake in the oven for about 20 minutes until golden.

 **6.** Then cut into slices and let the flapjacks cool in the tin.

☞ **Rabbit says always remember to wear oven gloves to hold a hot baking tin.**

1 Who is the **audience** for this recipe? (Think about the age group.)

2 How can you tell?

Password →

Audience

The **audience** is the people who read the text.

3 Look at the verbs. They are in a form called the imperative, which makes the sentences sound bossy. List the **imperative verbs** in the recipe.

Password →

Imperative verbs

Imperative verbs give commands. They keep the instructions short and simple.

For example, sentences without imperative verbs might read:
  You will need to get the sugar and measure out 2 tablespoons. Then you can add it to the flour and margarine.

But, sentences with imperative verbs might read:
  Measure out 2 tablespoons of sugar. *Add* it to the flour and margarine.

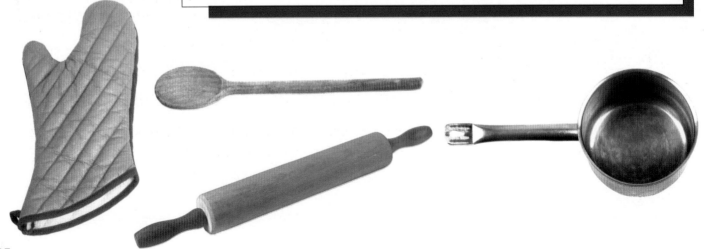

4 Copy out the following sentences and add the correct imperative verb from the list. Beware, as some of the verbs listed are not imperatives!

➤ First, ... your hands.
➤ .... out the shape.
➤ .... the chocolate.
➤ Next, ... the nuts.

> wash
> washed
> cut
> melting
> melt
> chop
> chopped
> add

5 Look back at the recipe. In which parts of the text does the writer include quantities and measurements?

6 Why does the writer number the steps in this recipe? (Think about **sequence**.)

Password →

Sequence

The **sequence** is the order.
Instructions need to be in sequence or they will confuse the reader.
For example, instructions for making a slice of toast should read:

➤ First place the bread in the toaster.
➤ Take it out when toasted.
➤ Butter the toast.

If you put these in a different order, the toast will be a disaster!

7 In instructions, adverbs add extra information about *how* a verb should be done. List the adverbs in the recipe, e.g. *gently*.

8 What else has the writer included to help the reader to make the flapjacks? (Look for pictures, lists, hints, etc.)

Instructions to make a 'Lava Light'

Read these instructions.

Make your own 'Lava Light'

What do I need?

- A glass jar or clear drinking glass
- Vegetable oil
- Salt
- Water
- Food colouring (if you want)

DANGER!
Don't forget to be careful with glass.

What do I do?

1 Pour about 3 inches of water into the jar.

2 Pour about 1/3 cup of vegetable oil into the jar. When everything settles, is the oil on top of the water or underneath it?

3 If you want, add one drop of food colouring to the jar. What happens? Is the drop in the oil or in the water? Does the colour spread?

4 Shake salt on top of the oil while you count slowly to 5. Wow! What happens to the food colouring? What happens to the salt?

5 Add more salt to keep the action going for as long as you want.

1 Have you seen other instructions to make things? Where? Discuss this with a partner.

2 Are these instructions written in a similar way to the recipe? Copy and complete the table below, giving examples of the features.

Feature	Flapjack	Lava Light
Title		
Audience		
Sub-headings		What do I need? What do I do?
Imperative verbs		
Measurements or quantities		
Sequence		
Pictures		
Adverbs	gently firmly	
Short, clear sentences		

Directions

Read the directions below. They were written to direct someone to a new sports centre but they got muddled up.

At the T-junction, turn left and walk down the hill.

Go past the Pizza Palace and the Post Office and follow the road for approximately 100 metres, until you reach a T-junction.

Finally, pass the garage on your right, and the Sports Centre is a bit further on, on the left.

Firstly, walk to the end of the street and turn left into Brown Lane.

Next, walk to the end of Brown Lane and turn right at the mini-roundabout. You should be able to see the Pizza Palace.

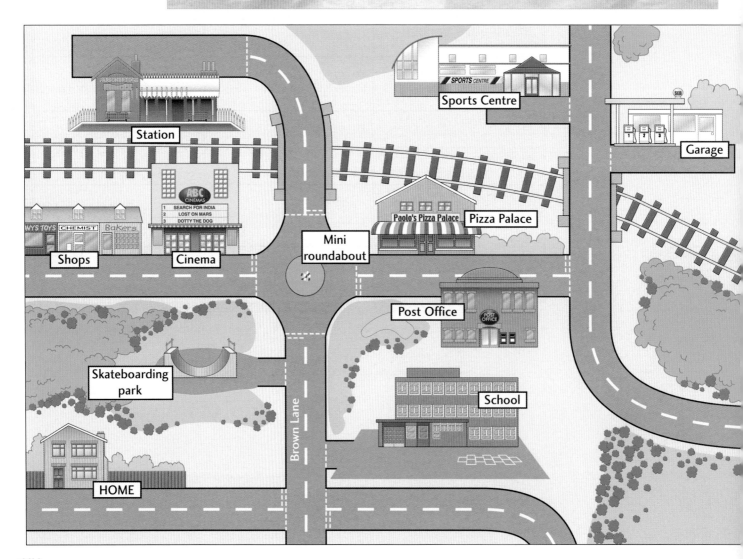

Look at the map. Then write the directions in the correct **sequence**.

2 List the words that helped you to sequence the directions. These words are called **connectives**.

Password →

Connectives

Connectives are words that link ideas together.

They can be used to **add** and **explain** ideas, e.g. *also, too, because, so, therefore*.
They can be used to **sequence** ideas, e.g. *first, next, then, before, after, finally*.

3 What land-marks helped you to put the directions into the correct order?

4 In pairs take it in turns to direct each other to school from your home, or to another place. (Don't forget to use imperatives.) You are giving instructions.

Round-up

You have learnt a great deal about instructions. List three things that you know are important when writing instructions.

Over to you

Have a go at writing a set of instructions. Choose what you want to write about. It could be one of these things:

➤ how to play a game
➤ how to send a text message
➤ how to put together a skateboard
➤ how to make something.

> → **Remember!**
>
> Instructions use:
> ➤ imperative verbs
> ➤ sequence (to show the right order)
> ➤ connectives.

Plan

Use this mind-map to help you plan your instructions.

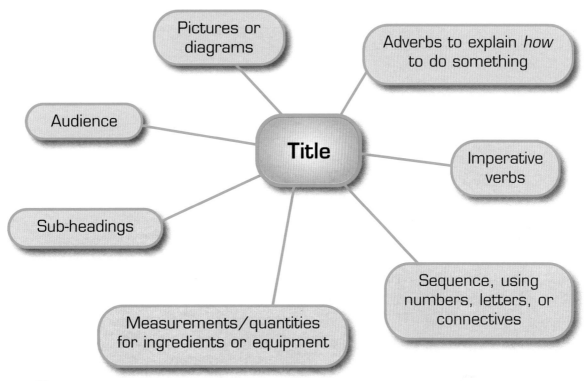

Follow these steps to write your instructions.

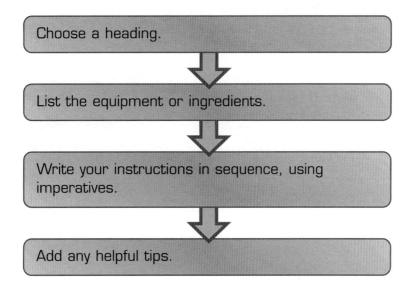

Persuasive texts

In this unit you will:

➤ look at the main features of persuasive texts (adverts in particular)
➤ write your own persuasive text.

Get started

Persuasive texts try to persuade (encourage) people to *do* or *think* something. For example, an advert tries to make you *buy* something; a campaign leaflet tries to make you *believe in* a particular idea.

Persuasive texts are all around us, on posters, adverts, leaflets, fliers, and in newspaper editorials. In this unit we are going to look in particular at adverts.

In pairs, think about the adverts that have caught your attention recently. Where were they? Make a list.

1. on a billboard (street poster)
2. on a department store carrier bag
3.
4.
5.

Adverts may try to catch our attention by being short, amusing and, most importantly, memorable. They often use **persuasive devices** to help us remember them.

Password ➔

Persuasive devices

Adverts use **persuasive devices** to make a strong impact on the reader. They might include:

➤ repetition ('*Hurry, hurry, hurry*, last day of sale!')
➤ exaggeration ('The *most precious gift* in the world')
➤ rhyme ('Bargains *galore* at The *Superstore*')
➤ alliteration (words starting with the same sounds, e.g. '*cool coats*')

 What persuasive devices do the following adverts use:

Beanz Meanz Heinz

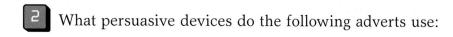

You can't get better than a Kwik-Fit fitter

You can do it when you B and Q it

3 Try to think up some rhyming adverts for:

➤ a fast, sporty car designed for young women
➤ a new tea bag made in Yorkshire
➤ a new brand of sportswear.

Keep the advert simple, but catchy.

Advert (1)

Read this advert.

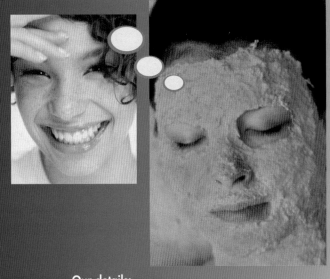

DREAM DIRT FACE PACK

Have you ever wondered how celebrities achieve that fresh look? How does their skin always look so silky and smooth? Then wonder no more! Dream Dirt Face Pack is the answer to your prayers!

If you want the softest, silkiest skin in your circle of friends, then buy one of our many face packs. Transform yourself easily and quickly in the privacy of your own bathroom. No need for expensive beauty salons.

After just 30 minutes, you will not only feel immensely pampered, but you will look like a million dollars.

So go on ladies, you deserve to be beautiful.

Our details:
Find out more about this amazing product.
Call and order on 08701 4455980

DON'T MISS OUT ON YOUR CHANCE TO STAND OUT!

1 Who do you think is the **audience** for this advert? Explain your answer.

Password → | **Audience**

The **audience** is the people who read the text.

2 What is this advert trying to persuade its audience to do? Discuss this with a partner and write down your thoughts.

3 Find the **rhetorical questions** in the advert.

> ➤ Do you think the writer expects the reader to answer them?
> ➤ Why do you think the writer includes them?

Be prepared to share your answers with the class.

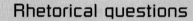
Password →

Rhetorical questions

A **rhetorical question** is a question that does not need an answer. It is often asked in a dramatic way, in order to draw attention to something.

For example, a teacher might see a student with his feet on the desk and say: 'Would you do that at home?' The teacher doesn't expect an answer, but is drawing attention to the poor behaviour.

4 Look at the following rhetorical questions. With a partner, try to work out what is meant by each question.

Rhetorical Question	Meaning
Can you turn your back on this poor defenceless animal, begging for a scrap of food?	
Now, who wouldn't want to drive an amazing car like this?	
Would you treat a member of your family in such a selfish way?	

5 Adverts often use **comparatives** and **superlatives** to describe a product. This makes the product sound more appealing and better than any other.

Look at the words in this panel. Sort them into two groups:
➤ comparatives
➤ superlatives.

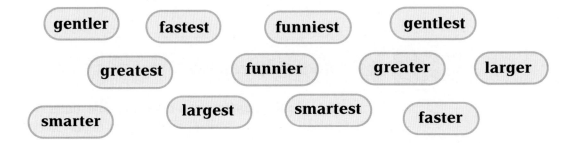

gentler   fastest   funniest   gentlest

greatest   funnier   greater   larger

smarter   largest   smartest   faster

Password →

Comparatives and superlatives

Comparatives state that one thing is better than another in some way, e.g. taller, faster.
Superlatives state that one thing is the best in that category, e.g. tallest, fastest.

6 Select two superlatives in the advert for the Dream Dirt Face Pack. Explain why you think the writer uses them.

7 This advert tries to persuade people that the face pack is a *cheap* way of looking 'like a million dollars'. How does it suggest this?

Advert (2)

Read this advert.

Words of Wisdom
by Rory Tyger

An enchanting collector plate – crafted in Royal Worcester fine porcelain

Actual size of plate is $7\frac{1}{2}$" in diameter.

When Newton encounters a bad-tempered bee, he doesn't panic – but remembers some words of wisdom!

A whimsical masterpiece – painted by a renowned artist

No one captures a teddy bear's appeal like renowned artist Rory Tyger. His masterpiece, **Words of Wisdom** is a charming work of art.

Newton is irresistible! As the bee alights on his nose, he recalls a time-honoured motto, "Keep calm at all times".

Exquisite quality – no quibble guarantee

Words of Wisdom has been preserved forever by Royal Worcester on their famous fine porcelain. Every plate will have a Certificate of Authenticity.

This plate is offered at just £19.95 (plus postage and handling). If you are not satisfied, simply return your plate within thirty days and owe nothing.

Words of Wisdom is the first plate in a new series entitled **Newton's Law**. Subscribers will have the opportunity, without obligation, to acquire the other plates in this enchanting collection.

Act now

Apply today. Send no money now! Call our order line now on **020 8391 2291**, or return your order form today, to:

Danbury Mint
Cox Lane, Chessington, Surrey KT9 1SE.

1 What type of **audience** do you think would be interested in this advert?

2 The advert is colourful and eye-catching. Why do you think that the designers have varied the shape, size and colour of the fonts in this advert?

3 Are there any instructions in the advert? (Remember, instructions tell people to do something. They are often used in persuasive texts.) List any that you find.

4 Instructions often use **imperative verbs**. Select the imperative verbs in the advert.

Password →

Imperative verbs

Imperative verbs give commands. They urge the reader to do something.

For example:
Buy now!
Pick up the phone and order...

5 Think of two more imperative verbs that could be used in adverts.

6 Persuasive texts often use powerful adjectives and adverbs. In adverts, they are used to emphasize the quality or performance of a product. List the adjectives and adverbs in the two adverts in this unit.

(Remember, adjectives describe nouns and adverbs describe verbs.)

	Dream Dirt Face Pack	Words of Wisdom
Adjectives		
Adverbs		

7 Which adjectives and adverbs do you feel are the most powerful? Explain the effect that they have.

8 Look at the sentences below.

a) The delicious food tasted like ...

b) The fantastic rollercoaster ride made me feel ...

c) The impressive, shiny car made the people on the street look and ...

d) The healthy diet eventually made me look like ...

➤ Copy out the sentences, and underline all the powerful adjectives that create a positive effect.
➤ Complete the sentences, keeping a positive tone.
➤ Next, replace each positive adjective with a negative one.
➤ Complete the sentences, continuing the negative tone.

For example:

The <u>delicious</u> food tasted like heaven.
The <u>disgusting</u> food tasted like poison.

9 Persuasive texts often use repetition to emphasize a key point or idea. Pick out repeated words or phrases in the Words of Wisdom advert. With a partner, talk about the effect of these repeated words.

10 Both adverts use the personal pronoun 'you'. How many examples can you find in each advert?

11 Writers often use 'you' in persuasive texts. With a partner, talk about why this might be. (Think about the tone of the text and the effect it has on the reader.)

Round-up

You have looked at many of the key features of persuasive texts. List three of the main features and give one example of each.

Over to you

Choose one idea from the list below and then plan and produce your own advert:

> ➤ a new breakfast cereal that includes both chocolate and fruit
> ➤ the latest designer sunglasses
> ➤ a quick-drying nail polish that changes colour during the day
> ➤ a pen with invisible ink.

→ Remember!

Persuasive texts use:
> ➤ repetition
> ➤ exaggeration
> ➤ rhetorical questions
> ➤ imperatives.

Plan

Use a grid like the one below to help you plan your advert. Remember to make your advert short, fun and memorable.

Writing prompts	Notes
What I am advertising	
Who my audience is	
The most important feature (selling point) of my product	
Imperative verbs that I'll use	
A rhetorical question	
Comparatives and superlatives (things to exaggerate)	
Rhyme and alliteration	
Powerful adjectives and adverbs	
Colours, fonts and pictures	

 Now produce your advert.

In this unit you will:

➤ look at how discursive texts set out different points
➤ write a discursive text with clear points on each side.

Get started

When was the last time you talked about a film or a TV programme with a friend? When was the last time you talked to an adult about something you wanted to do? When two or more people put forward their views and answer each other, then that is a discussion. When a discussion is written down, it is called a **discursive text**.

Pick one of the topics below and discuss it as a class. Listen carefully to different opinions.

The best type of music

The most entertaining TV soap

The most skilled football team

The best teacher

A short discursive text

Read this discursive text.

Should there be longer winter holidays?

Experiments will be carried out this year to find out if students will benefit from longer school holidays in the winter.

At the moment, the Christmas holiday is only two weeks in most schools. Some people think this is too short. They argue the short holiday means students have to suffer too many dark mornings in term-time, and poorly heated schools for much of the winter. In addition, they argue that longer holidays would help to cut accidents caused by travelling to school in poor weather conditions. They also think longer holidays would help schools to cut their heating bills.

However, some people fear that more lessons missed in winter will damage learning. Another argument against longer school holidays in the winter is that it would mean having shorter holidays in the summer. Many parents are against this because it is when some families take their annual holiday.

If successful, this experiment may be made law, and all students will get extra holidays during winter months.

1 Find examples of two different viewpoints in the **discursive text** that you have just read:

a) people who are *for* longer winter holidays

b) people who are *against* longer winter holidays.

Copy and complete the grid below, listing the arguments for and against.

For longer winter holidays	Against longer winter holidays
Will reduce number of dark mornings in term-time	

Password ➔

Discursive text

A **discursive text** is a discussion, written down.

2 Which side do you agree with? Explain your views to the class.

Get started

You are now going to look at two texts. Each one has a different viewpoint on skateboarding. Then you will look at how a discursive text looks at both viewpoints together.

A viewpoint against skateboarding

SKATEBOARD DAMAGE OF £20,000

DAMAGE caused by skateboarding youngsters on Bridlington's showpiece South Promenade has left ratepayers with a possible £20,000 repair bill.

In a no-nonsense warning, Alan Menzies the head of East Yorkshire Tourism Office said the authority intended to pursue illegal skateboarders and make them pay for the damage they had done. 'We will use CCTV film to identify the culprits, pursue those who cause damage and make them pay for it.'

Emergency work has begun on temporary repairs to make safe the cracked and jagged blocks and tiles around the children's paddling pool before the Easter holiday.

Mr Menzies added that skateboarders were also a hazard to people using the promenade and there had been instances when people had said they felt threatened by the youths.

Adapted from an article by Alan Brook, in *Bridlington Free Press*

1 Skim read the text to pick out:

➤ what the headline says
➤ the name of the head of the Tourist Office
➤ how the people causing damage will be identified.

2 Now pick out the following **facts**:

➤ how much money it could cost to repair the damage
➤ what damage has been caused by skateboarding
➤ what other problem, apart from damage, is caused by skateboarders.

Password →

Facts

Facts are something that can be proved to be true.

For example:
➤ the colour of someone's eyes
➤ the amount of money in a wallet
➤ the price of a CD.

3 Why does the writer say how much it will cost to repair the damage?

a) so that people will send in donations to help pay for it
b) because it shows how expensive skateboarding is as a hobby
c) in order to shock adults who pay rates (local taxes)

(Choose the correct answer.)

4 By mentioning 'the children's paddling pool' what is the writer trying to make the readers feel? (Think about young children in a pool that has cracked and broken tiles before you answer this!)

5 Think about the words 'hazard', 'illegal' and 'culprits'. What images and ideas do these words create?

A viewpoint in favour of skateboarding

Is Skateboarding a Crime?

Skateboarding is great fun. It teaches balance, co-ordination and muscle control, and rewards the learner for persistence and effort. Every goal set and achieved is a marvellous life lesson. Where would any of us be if we didn't reach that little bit farther, try just a little bit harder?

The element of danger, or risk, appeals to a certain something within us. Sports with a challenge and the potential for hurting oneself attract those who thrive on adrenalin. I'm not going to put people down for enjoying the thrill of those sports.

There just aren't enough skate parks around for the number of skaters. Some places have skate parks mainly because the teenagers in that area organized to get one. Unfortunately, the down side is that some parks aren't used, so city and park officials hesitate to build more. As an example, there's a skateboard 'bowl' in Frederick Street Park, but for all the times I've been there with my grandsons, I can count on one hand the skaters I've seen using it. They seem to prefer the freedom of the streets, the thrill of jumping 'natural' obstacles such as steps, curbs, whatever.

So, is skateboarding a crime? Of course not. It is dangerous, exhilarating, fun and sometimes a nuisance, but a crime? No.

Adapted from *www.santacruz.about.com*

1 Scan the text to find these words:

➤ persistence
➤ adrenalin
➤ exhilarating

Write down what they mean in *your own words*. (You may need a dictionary.)

2 Who does the author say has organized skate parks in some places? Choose from the ideas below:

a) city and park officials
b) local teenagers
c) grandparents.

3 Look at the **opinions** of the author.

➤ What does the author think that young people *learn* from skateboarding?
➤ Why does the author think some places *don't* have skate parks?
➤ Pick out *three* adjectives which show his views of skateboarding? (Remember, an adjective describes a noun.)

Password | **Opinions**

An **opinion** is someone's view, e.g. about who the best footballer is, what the best sort of holiday is, which clothes look cool. (Compare this with **facts**, which can be proven.)

4 Talk about what the author is trying to make the reader think.

➤ Why is there a lot about the excitement you can get from skateboarding?
➤ Why does the author mention going to a skate 'bowl' with his grandsons?
➤ Why does the article begin and end with the same question?

Get started

In a discursive text, you need to look at both sides of an argument. This means contrasting both viewpoints in one text.

1 Refer to the two texts about skateboarding you have read. Copy and complete the grid below. It will help you to contrast the arguments for and against skateboarding.

	SKATEBOARD DAMAGE OF £20,000	Is Skateboarding a Crime?
Words used to describe skateboarding or skateboarders	hazard illegal culprits	fun
Attitudes of people to skateboarders (either the writer or people in the article)		
Feelings the article makes the reader have about skateboarders		
How the pictures and layout make the article interesting to read		

2 Which of the attitudes in these articles do *you* agree with? Explain your opinion to a partner and give reasons for it.

A discursive text about skateboarding

In this discursive text, the writer puts forward both points of view on skateboarding, then gives her own opinion.

Should skateboarding in public places be banned?

Much has been written in newspapers recently about the problems to do with skateboarding in public places. Less has been said about the positive side of the sport. It's time that both points of view are considered fairly.

Skateboarding has become more popular over recent years after it arrived in the UK from the USA. However, unlike America, we in Britain have fewer places properly equipped for skateboarders so they use any space they can find to provide a challenge. Kerbs, benches, plinths, seats – all have been used as places to practise their skills. This has resulted in thousands of pounds of damage and skateboarders being branded as vandals. Some councils have banned skateboarding in specific areas due to the high costs of repairing the damage they have caused. One council reported £20,000 worth of repairs being needed. People, understandably, do not want skateboarders around for fear of what might happen.

On the other hand, it must be pointed out that skateboarding is a far better, and healthier way of spending time than some other activities young people could become involved in. For one thing, the exercise helps their bodies stay healthy. It is a social sport with competition being fairly friendly and positive, which again is good for young people. In addition, it is also a low-risk sport – far fewer injuries are caused by skateboarding than some other sports, for example, soccer. The fact that so many skateboarders use the streets is mainly due to the shortage of proper facilities for them.

In conclusion, I would suggest that if councils really want to solve the problem of skateboarders causing damage, they should provide parks for them to use which would be a permanent area for the sport. This would have the bonus of keeping young people off the streets as well as saving the public areas from damage.

1 Look at how the writer has organized this discursive text. Each paragraph has a clear purpose, with main points. Copy and complete the grid below.

	Main points	Effective words/ phrases used
First paragraph – introduction	➤ Sets out topic for discussion	'much', 'less', 'both points of view'
Second paragraph – points against	➤ Skaters use streets ➤	
Third paragraph – points in favour	➤ ➤ ➤	'friendly and positive'
Fourth paragraph – conclusion	➤ ➤ ➤	

2 In a discursive text, it is important that the reader is given 'signposts' in the text, so they know when there is a change of viewpoint. **Connectives** are a type of signpost. List the connectives in this text.

 Password →

Connectives

Connectives are words that link parts of a text together. They help a writer to organize his or her ideas, and help a reader to understand the direction of the text.

For example: *first, however, next, on the other hand, although, since.*

3 Below is a plan for a discursive text, but the paragraphs are muddled up. Put them into the correct order.

Conclusion sums up the arguments and gives writer's opinion.

Text argues for the issue.

Introduction says what the text is about.

Text argues against the issue.

Round-up

Now you should have a good idea of what discursive texts are and how they are organized. With a partner, see if you can remember what the following words mean:

➤ discursive text
➤ facts
➤ opinions
➤ connectives.

(Look back in the Password panels to check your answers!)

Over to you

Now try writing a discursive text of your own. Choose a topic or use one of these questions to discuss:

➤ Are films better than books?
➤ Are pop/sports stars over-paid?
➤ Should parents set a time for teenagers to be home at night?

Remember!

Discursive texts need:
➤ an introduction to the topic
➤ two or more points of view
➤ facts and opinions
➤ connectives
➤ a conclusion that includes the writer's opinion.

Plan

Use this plan to organize your discursive text.

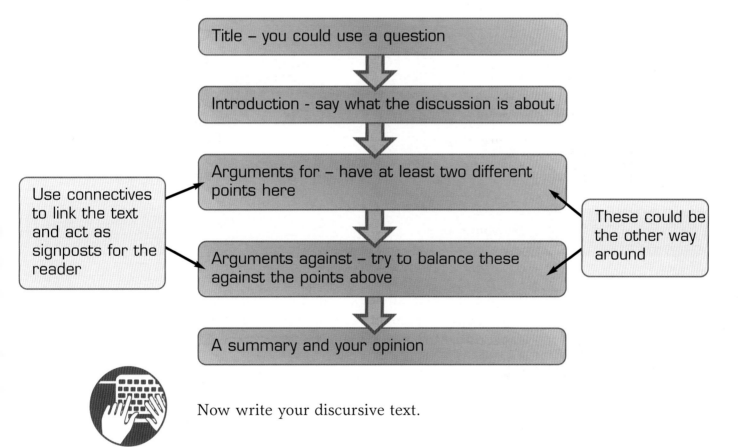

Title – you could use a question

Introduction - say what the discussion is about

Arguments for – have at least two different points here

Use connectives to link the text and act as signposts for the reader

These could be the other way around

Arguments against – try to balance these against the points above

A summary and your opinion

Now write your discursive text.

In this unit you will:

➤ explore a range of advice texts
➤ identify the main features of an advice text
➤ write informal advice that is easy for the reader to act on.

Get started

We give and take advice all the time, often without being aware of it. For example, we might read some advice in a teenage magazine or a teacher might sit us down and give us some advice. Advice can be written down or verbal.

Advice should give support, guidance and reassurance. Advice texts are usually a mix of information, instruction, explanation and persuasion.

1 In pairs, brainstorm possible answers to these questions:

➤ Who might give you advice and when?
➤ When might you give advice to another person?
➤ Where might you find advice written down?

2 List ten topics that could be the basis of an advice text.

1. How to look after a rabbit.
2. How to revise for a test.
3. How to eat a healthy, balanced diet.
4.
5.
6.
7.
8.
9.
10.

Advice on dating

Read the text on page 72. It gives advice on how to increase your chances of getting the date that you want!

1 Who do you think is the **audience** for this text? Give reasons for your answer.

Password →

Audience

The **audience** is the people who read the text.

2 Where do you think you might find this sort of advice text?:

a) in an old people's home
b) on a school notice-board
c) in a magazine for teenagers
d) in a doctor's surgery
(Choose the right answer.)

Get smart: get your date!

We've all been there. Crying into our pillows at night because the love of our life fails, day after day, week after week, to notice us! Boo hoo! Well, kids, that really would be a crying shame … especially if you were to just sit there, accept this pitiful fate and do nothing to make your dream come true! So, comrades in the battle of love … sit back, take note of these three tried and tested snippets of advice … and watch the person of your dreams walk straight into your arms – or at least into the local café to buy you a milk shake!

Hint 1
Make sure you brush your teeth every day!
That first, potential kiss could be but moments away. Surely, you don't want to frighten them away by turning their hair yellow as you lean in for that tender moment. Halitosis, my friends, is not recommended!

Hint 2
Get into Feng Shui!
According to Chinese beliefs, how your room and possessions are laid out and positioned can determine the fate in your life. However, for the purpose of this topic, the main message is … tidy your room! You never know when that special someone will pop over to do homework with you. (Oh, and make sure your dirty socks are not on show.)

Hint 3
Long term financial projections!
Yes, the most important advice of all. So what does it mean? Well, to you philistines out there, it means make sure you have a little bit of 'dosh' on you at all times, just in case you have to buy your dream mate a bag of crisps without them giving you prior warning!

Well kiddies, that's it! Simple but effective! Three steps to ensure you get your dream date. Hygiene, appearance and a bit of ready cash will blend into your very own cocktail of successful dating! Or, if not, you can always use that bit of money to go out and buy a good old bag of chips!

3 List any specialist words in this text. Your list might begin like this:

> • hygiene
> • Feng Shui

(If you are not sure what some of the words mean, look them up in a dictionary. Then, write them in your own spelling log.)

4 In pairs, talk about exactly what these words mean in this advice text. Then, write new sentences using these words.

5 What '**person**' is this text written in? Is it first, second or third person?

Password →

Person

Text can be written in different forms of **person**.

For example:
  I have clean teeth. (first person)
  You tidied your room. (second person)
  He/she has money. (third person)

The second person is used to address the reader, 'you', directly. It is also used in imperative verbs (without the 'you') in instructions.

6 How would you describe the **tone** of this advice text? Talk about it with a partner.

Discuss the effect of:
➤ the exclamation marks
➤ the way the reader is addressed
➤ the slang words
➤ the expression 'a crying shame'.

Password →

Tone

The **tone** is the mood of the text.

For example:
A *formal tone* is used for serious texts, such as what to do in emergencies. A formal tone is polite, clear and precise.
An *informal tone* is used for light-hearted texts, such as comic ideas on what clothes to wear. An informal tone is chatty, uses casual words and feels like a conversation with a friend.

7 When might advice texts use a serious, formal tone? (Think about different subjects).

Advice from the NSPCC

Read the advice text on page 75. It is from the NSPCC web site.

Who do you think is the **audience** for this text? Be prepared to explain your answer.

How would you describe the **tone** of this text?

a) funny
b) formal
c) light-hearted
d) serious
e) informal

(Choose one or more descriptions.)

Advice on surfing safely

Chat rooms and messaging can be great fun, but remember, you never really know who you are talking to online. It could be someone trying to trick you, some kind of weirdo, or someone really dangerous.

To make sure you are safe:

- **Never use your real name** in chat rooms – pick a special online nickname.

- **Never ever tell anyone personal things about yourself or your family** – like your address or telephone number, or the school or clubs you go to. That goes for sending them photos as well (that way if you don't want to hear from them again, you only have to log off). Remember, even if somebody tells you about themselves, never tell them things about you.

If you arrange to meet up with someone you've only spoken to online, remember that they **might not** be **who** they said they were, so **only meet people in public places and take along an adult** – they should do this too, because they don't know who you really are either!

Never respond to nasty or rude messages, and never send any either! If you feel suspicious or uncomfortable about the way a conversation is going, or if it's getting really personal, save a record of it and stop the conversation there and then. That way you can show someone and ask what they think.

Be careful with any email attachments or links that people send you, they might contain nasty images, or computer 'viruses' that could ruin your PC. So if you don't know who it's from, definitely don't open it.

Avoid sites that are meant for adults. You might be curious, but sometimes these sites can be difficult to get out of, they can cost more on the phone bill, and they can detect your email address and start sending you stuff you really don't want to get. And if you see rude pictures where they shouldn't be, always let an adult know so they can get them removed.

Agree some rules with your parents or carers about what you can and can't do on the Net. It'll save arguments later. You probably know more about using it than they do, though, so make sure they know what they're agreeing to!

Don't let it take over your life! Keep up your other interests and try and use the Internet with friends and family, not just on your own.

3 Select examples of words or phrases that helped you to decide on the tone of the text. Be prepared to feed back your findings to the class.

4 Many advice texts use instructions. The grid below lists the main features of instructions. Copy it out and tick the features that you can find in the NSPCC advice text.

Features of instructions	NSPCC text
Imperative verbs (these sound bossy!)	
A clear sequence	
Connectives	
Present tense	
Aimed at a specific audience	

5 Select four examples of imperative verbs. With a partner, talk about why imperatives work well in advice texts.

6 Advice texts need to be clear. Writers often use **simple sentences** in advice texts to make their message clear to the reader. Find a simple sentence in the NSPCC advice text.

Password →

Simple sentences

A **simple sentence** contains one subject and one verb.

For example:

You should eat vegetables.

subject   verb

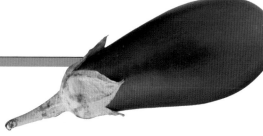

7 Advice texts often need to give quite a lot of detail and information. Writers often present this in **complex sentences**. Find three complex sentences in the NSPCC text.

Password →

Complex sentences

A **complex sentence** has a *main clause* and at least one *subordinate clause*.
➤ A *main clause* makes sense on its own. It can form a sentence.
➤ A *subordinate clause* does not make sense on its own. It depends on the main clause.

For example:

Even though you might feel fine, you should try to stay warm and dry.

subordinate clause   main clause

8 How many times can you find the connective (linking word) 'or' in the NSPCC advice text? Advice texts often use connectives to give the reader choices or more than one example.

9 List four examples of what 'or' connects in this advice text.

77

Round-up

With a partner, list four things that you now know about advice texts.

Over to you

At the start of this unit you listed some topics for advice texts. Choose one of these and write a piece of advice for a friend or relative.

> **Remember!**
>
> Advice texts:
> ➤ use a mix of instruction, persuasion, explanation and information
> ➤ are written for a particular audience
> ➤ often use the second person ('you')
> ➤ use a tone suited to the topic and audience.

Plan

Use a mind-map to prompt your thinking.

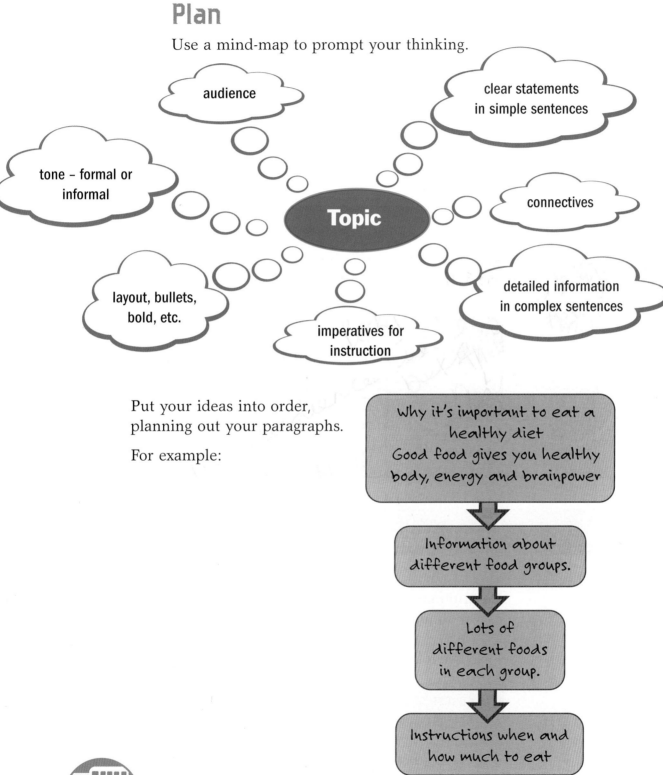

audience

clear statements in simple sentences

tone – formal or informal

connectives

Topic

layout, bullets, bold, etc.

detailed information in complex sentences

imperatives for instruction

Put your ideas into order, planning out your paragraphs.

For example:

Why it's important to eat a healthy diet
Good food gives you healthy body, energy and brainpower

Information about different food groups.

Lots of different foods in each group.

Instructions when and how much to eat

Now write your advice text in full.

In this unit you will:

➤ look at how writers convey setting, character and mood through description
➤ describe an object or person in detail.

Get started

Descriptions give detail about people, places, objects and events. They can be found in fiction and non-fiction texts.

Read the following description:

The house had been supposedly empty for years, so who or what was making the faint moans I could hear so clearly? Despite my desperation to leave this dark, damp dwelling, I knew I had to unfold the mystery that surrounded it. As I nervously approached the front door, I noticed, for the first time, a shadow lurking in the window of an upstairs room.

With a partner, talk about:

> ➤ where you might expect to read something like this
> ➤ what mood the writer is trying to create
> ➤ what helped you to answer these questions.

Language is the key to descriptive writing. When writers describe a person, object or setting, they choose their words and craft their sentences very carefully.

Describing a character's looks

Writers describe their characters in detail to make the reader feel that they know them, and to draw the reader into the story. Specific details help the reader to imagine what the character looks like.

In this text, J.K. Rowling introduces the character Hagrid, in *Harry Potter and the Philosopher's Stone*.

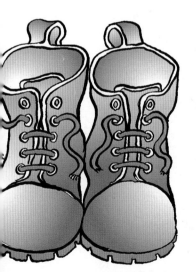

> If the motorbike was huge, it was nothing to the man sitting astride it. He was almost twice as tall as a normal man and at least five times as wide. He looked simply too big to be allowed, and so wild – long tangles of bushy black hair and beard hid most of his face, he had hands the size of dustbin lids and his feet in their leather boots were like baby dolphins. In his vast, muscular arms he was holding a bundle of blankets.

1. To emphasize how huge Hagrid is, the author uses a **simile** to compare Hagrid to a normal man. She states that he was 'twice as tall' and 'at least five times as wide'. Write down another simile that J.K. Rowling uses in this extract. What effect does this simile have?

Password →

Similes

A **simile** helps the reader to imagine something by comparing it to something else. Similes often include the words 'like' or 'as', e.g. *as soft as butter*.

2 Copy and complete the following similes:

➤ as white as _____
➤ as sly as a _____
➤ as hard as _____
➤ as busy as _____
➤ as cold as _____

3 To make descriptions interesting and detailed, writers often use **noun phrases**. J.K. Rowling doesn't just state that Hagrid had hair, she describes it as 'long tangles of bushy black hair'. This helps the reader to picture Hagrid. Copy and complete this table by adding the noun phrases from the text.

Noun phrase	Noun
Long tangles of bushy black hair	hair
	hands
	boots
	arms

Password →

Noun phrases

A **noun phrase** is a group of words that describe, and include, a noun. They give more information about a noun.

For example:
A sleek new sports car, tells us that the car is smooth, shiny, new and sporty.

4 Noun phrases can be just one or two words, or a long phrase. Try adding detail to the following nouns to make noun phrases. (Hint: you may find it helpful to ask yourself the question – what does it look like? Use the picture to help you with the first noun.)

Copy and complete the table.

Noun phrase	Noun
	dungeon
	tree
	trainers
	teacher

So far, we've looked at nouns at the end of noun phrases. However, some nouns are put at the beginning of noun phrases. For example, if the noun phrase uses a **preposition**, to tell you where the noun is, the noun comes first, e.g. *the car on the bridge*.

Password →

Prepositions

Prepositions tell you *where* something is, e.g. *under, on, by, at, in, across, behind, down, over*.

Prepositions can also tell you *when* something is, e.g. on Tuesday, *at* 9am.

5 Take the noun phrases that you wrote in the last table and develop them by adding detail after the noun. Start with a preposition. For example: The cold, dark dungeon *under the castle*.
(Hint: You may find it helpful to ask yourself: *where* is this?)

Clues about personality

In a story, a reader needs to know about a character's personality as well as their looks.

Read the following extract from *There's A Boy In The Girls' Bathroom* by Louis Sachar.

> There are some kids – you can tell just by looking at them – who are good spitters. That is probably the best way to describe Bradley Chalkers. He looked like a good spitter.
>
> He was the oldest and the toughest-looking kid in Mrs Ebbel's class. He was a year older than the other kids. That was because he had taken the fourth grade twice. Now he was in the fifth grade for the first, but probably not the last, time.
>
> Jeff stared at him, then gave him a dollar and ran away.
>
> Bradley laughed to himself, then watched all the other kids have fun.
>
> When he returned to class after recess, he was surprised Mrs Ebbel didn't say anything to him. He figured that Jeff would probably tell on him and that he'd have to give back the dollar.
>
> He sat at his desk in the back of the room – last seat, last row. *He's afraid to tell on me*, he decided. *He knows if he tells on me, I'll punch his face in!* He laughed to himself.
>
> He ate lunch alone too.

A good writer may not tell the reader directly about a character's personality. The writer might prefer the reader to **infer and deduce** what the character is like by reading the clues.

Infer and deduce

Infer means to form an opinion.
Deduce means to draw a conclusion from the information given.

For example, a detective needs to *infer* who the murderer is and *deduce* what happened from clues at the scene of a crime.

1 When you infer and deduce, you need to look closely at the text and think carefully about the clues the writer is giving you. For example, think about these clues:

➤ Clue 1 – 'He ate his lunch alone too.'
➤ Clue 2 – 'then watched all the other kids have fun.'

What do these clues tell us about Bradley? (Think about friends.)

2 With a partner, talk about what you think Bradley is like as a person. Give examples from the extract to support your views. The following questions may help you:

➤ What do you think the writer is implying by describing Bradley as a 'good spitter'?
➤ Do you think Bradley is happy?
➤ What do you think Bradley is like in lessons?

Now join up with another pair and share your ideas.

3 Good description uses different types of sentences. Find an example from the text of:

a) a simple sentence
b) a **compound sentence**
c) a **complex sentence**.

Password →

Compound sentences

A **compound sentence** is made up of two main clauses, joined by *and*, *or*, *but* or *so*.

For example:

He kicked the ball, and it smashed through the glass.

main clause   main clause

Password →

Complex sentences

A **complex sentence** is made up of a *main clause* (that makes sense on its own) and one or more *subordinate clauses* (which depends on the main clause).

For example:

Whilst waiting for the bus, Tom thought about the match.

subordinate clause   main clause

4 Write out this complex sentence from the extract:

> 'When he returned to class after recess, he was surprised Mrs Ebbel didn't say anything to him.'

Underline the subordinate clause.

5 Subordinate clauses can come before or after the main clause. Writers vary the position, depending on what they wish to emphasize. Rewrite the following complex sentences by changing the position of the subordinate clauses. (You may wish to add a comma to the first sentence.)

a) James felt relieved when the final whistle blew.
b) Before the delivery arrived, Janet finished the painting.
c) Despite her best efforts, Nicole could not beat the record.

Describing an object

Description can focus on objects as well as people. Look at the following extract from Roald Dahl's *The Hitch-hiker*.

I had a new car. It was an exciting toy, a big BMW 3.3 Li, which means 3.3 litre, long wheelbase, fuel injection. It had a top speed of 129 m.p.h. and terrific acceleration. The body was pale blue. The seats inside were darker blue and they were made of leather, genuine soft leather of the finest quality. The windows were electrically operated and so was the sun-roof. The radio aerial popped up when I switched on the radio, and disappeared when I switched it off. The powerful engine growled and grunted impatiently at slow speeds, but at sixty miles an hour the growling stopped and the motor began to purr with pleasure.

1 With a partner, discuss why you think Roald Dahl uses the word 'toy' to describe the car.

2 Look at the verbs that describe the car's engine, e.g. 'growled', 'grunted'. What else might you describe using these verbs?

3 When a writer describes something as if it is alive (even though it is not), it is called *personification*. Can you find one more example?

4 Adverbs are often used in descriptions. They give more information about verbs, e.g. 'grunted *impatiently*'. Pair up the following verbs and adverbs:

Note that many adverbs end in –ly.

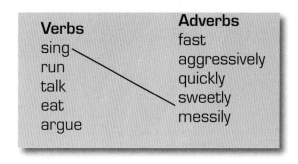

Verbs
sing
run
talk
eat
argue

Adverbs
fast
aggressively
quickly
sweetly
messily

5 Scan the text on page 87 to find five adjectives. List them. (Remember, adjectives describe nouns.)

6 In this extract, Roald Dahl uses short sentences as well as longer, more complex ones. What effect do the short sentences have?

Round-up

With a partner, talk about what you have learnt in this unit. Choose four features (writing techniques) that you would use in a description. Share your ideas with the rest of the class and decide on the most powerful features of description.

Over to you

Now try writing your own description of a person. He or she could be:

➤ a friend
➤ a member of your family
➤ an imaginary character (use the pictures below to give you ideas).

Describe your character's personality as well as what they look like. (Remember that you are writing about the person, not about their life.)

Remember!

Descriptions use:
➤ noun phrases
➤ similes
➤ clues for the reader to infer and deduce
➤ a variety of sentence types.

Plan

First, plan your description. Draw up five boxes, with the headings used below. Then add your own notes using the bulleted points as prompts.

Physical features

➤ Choose the most interesting physical features to describe, which reveal most about the character.
➤ Use similes, e.g. *his eyes were as dark as coal*.
➤ Add detail by including noun phrases, e.g. *his tanned, muscular arms*.

Personality

➤ Try to give the reader clues, so they can infer and deduce.

Actions

➤ Choose interesting, unusual verbs.
➤ Use adverbs for extra detail.

Variety of sentences

➤ Short sentences can be very effective.
➤ Remember to vary the position of the subordinate clause in complex sentences.
➤ Remember to use the third person.

Speech

➤ What the character says.
➤ How the character says it.

Now write your description in full.

In this unit you will:

➤ look at the structure and layout of playscripts
➤ look at how playwrights build up characters and settings
➤ write a short piece of playscript.

Miss, we think you'd be good as Dracula.

Get started

Can you think of any plays you have read? There may not be many, because we tend to watch plays, rather than read them. However, all plays have to start on the page. They are written in a special way, so that the actors know who says what, when and how.

In this unit we will look at the layout of playscripts (how they are written down). We will also look at how playwrights build up their characters and settings to create strong moods and atmosphere.

Layout of playscripts

Read these two extracts. They are both from a story by Terry Pratchett, called *Johnny and the Dead*. One is from the novel and one is from the playscript.

The two boys walked through the cemetery now, kicking up the drifts of fallen leaves.

'It's Halloween next week,' said Wobbler.

'I'm having a disco. You have to come as something horrible. Don't bother to find a disguise.'

'Thanks,' said Johnny.

'You notice how there's a lot more Halloween stuff in the shops these days?' said Wobbler.

'It's because of Bonfire Night,' said Johnny. 'Too many people were blowing themselves up with fireworks, so they invented Halloween, where you just wear masks and stuff.'

'Mrs Nugent says all that sort of thing is tampering with the occult,' said Wobbler. Mrs Nugent was the Johnsons' next door neighbour, and known to be unreasonable on subjects like Madonna played at full volume at 3 a.m.

'Probably it is,' said Johnny.

'She says witches are abroad on Halloween,' said Wobbler.

'What?' Johnny's forehead wrinkled. 'Like ... Majorca and places?'

'Suppose so,' said Wobbler.

Wobbler and Johnny walking

Wobbler It's Hallowe'en next week. I'm having a party; you have to come as something horrible. So don't bother to find a disguise.

Johnny Thanks.

Wobbler You notice how there's a lot more Halloween stuff in the shops these days?

Johnny It's because of Bonfire Night. Too many people were blowing themselves up with fireworks, so they invented Hallowe'en, where you just wear masks and stuff.

Wobbler My mum's friend, Mrs Nugent, says all that sort of thing is tampering with the occult.

Johnny Probably is.

Wobbler She says witches are abroad on Hallowe'en.

Johnny What ...? Like... Majorca, and places?

Wobbler *[Not very certain on this point]* 'Spose so.

Both extracts tell the same part of the story, but which is from the novel and which is from the playscript?
(Hint: imagine that you are an actor in the play. In which text is it easiest to see who says what?)

2 Most of the spoken words are the same in both texts, but how are they laid out differently?
(Hint: look at the punctuation and line spaces.)

3 Look at the **stage directions** in the playscript. Why does the playwright need to put them in?

a) Because the characters have to say these words.
b) Because they tell the actors what to do on stage.
c) Because they tell the actors how to say their lines.
(Choose two right answers.)

Password →

Stage directions

Stage directions are written (*usually in italics*) in playscripts for the actors.

➤ They give instructions on actions, scenery and props.
For example:
> **Jake**: *[clenching his fist]* Don't come near me
> *Wendy and Josh enter, carrying Ewan.*
> *The lights go down.*

➤ They tell the actors what mood or tone they should speak in.
For example:
> **Sam**: *[angrily]* Where are you going?

4 Here is another extract from the novel. Johnny wants to talk to one of the dead, so he knocks at the big tomb of Alderman Thomas Bowler.

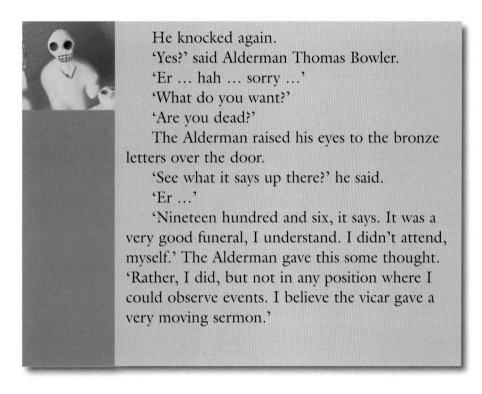

He knocked again.

'Yes?' said Alderman Thomas Bowler.

'Er … hah … sorry …'

'What do you want?'

'Are you dead?'

The Alderman raised his eyes to the bronze letters over the door.

'See what it says up there?' he said.

'Er …'

'Nineteen hundred and six, it says. It was a very good funeral, I understand. I didn't attend, myself.' The Alderman gave this some thought. 'Rather, I did, but not in any position where I could observe events. I believe the vicar gave a very moving sermon.'

Turn this text into playscript. You will need to think about:

➤ what the Alderman says
➤ what Johnny says
➤ stage directions to describe actions
➤ stage directions to describe mood or tone.

Use this model to help you lay out your playscript:

stage direction
Character 1 What he says.
Character 2 What he says.
Character 1 What he says.
Character 2 What he says.
stage direction
Character 1 What he says.
Character 2 What he says.
Character 1 What he says.

Characters

Playwrights build their characters by:

➤ what they say
➤ what they do
➤ showing how others treat them.

Read the extract on page 95. It is from a play based on the novel *Dracula* by Bram Stoker. This scene is a meeting between Dracula and Renfield, a human slave to Dracula, who wishes to be a full vampire.

Renfield   I am of your kind –

Dracula   No! You are not of my kind! You shall never be! You are – as you are. Be content with it.

Renfield   No!

Suddenly, Dracula grabs Renfield by the throat.

Dracula   No? You would say no to me! You would dare! You know how I could crush you, little man. Crush you out of all existence, like one of those insects you feed upon. It would mean nothing to me. You live because I choose you to live. And if I choose you to die – you die.

He squeezes Renfield's throat, choking him. Then, he throws him down to the floor. Renfield gasps.

Dracula   There. I choose you to live – for now. And I give you something. Your freedom.

Renfield   Freedom?

Dracula   To leave this place. Your attendants sleep. The door to your cell is open. Your path is clear. Go.

Renfield now realizes that Dracula has abandoned him. He speaks in despair.

Renfield   Go? Go where? Where would I go? What is there for me out there?

This extract shows us a lot about Dracula's character. He is not simply evil – he is more complex than that.

1 What does Dracula mean when he says Renfield is 'not of my kind'?

2 Dracula tells Renfield to be 'content' with what he is. What does he mean by that?

   a) That Renfield should be quiet as he is getting on Dracula's nerves.

   b) That being human is not that bad really.

   c) That being a vampire is actually terrible – and it is better to stay human.

   (Choose the right answer.)

3 Do you think that Dracula is happy or unhappy? Talk about this to a partner and give reasons for your answer.

4 What does Dracula do and say that shows us he enjoys feeling his power?

   Use this sentence to help you write your answer:

> We can see that Dracula enjoys his feeling of power when he says, '...' and when he ...

5 One word in the stage directions describes Renfield's mood. Which one is it?

6 Who do you think is the **audience** for this play? Give a reason for your answer.

Password →

Audience

The **audience** is the people who read the text or watch the play or film.

Here is another extract from *Johnny and the Dead*. Johnny is taking his friends down to the graveyard. Read it carefully.

Bigmac produces a sharpened stake and hammer.

Johnny Bigmac!

Bigmac Well, you never know …

Johnny Leave them here!

Bigmac Oh, all right.

Bigmac puts down the hammer and the stake.

Yo-less Anyway, it's not stakes for ghosts. That's for vampires.

Wobbler (*Not much reassured by this*) Oh, thank you!

Johnny Look, this is just the cemetery. It's not Transylvania! There's just dead people here! Dead people are just people who were living once! A few years ago they were just mowing lawns and putting up Christmas decorations and being people's grandparents. There's nothing to be frightened of!

Yo-less Yes … It's peaceful, isn't it?

Bigmac Quiet as the grave. (*He laughs*)

1 What shows us that Bigmac takes note of what Johnny says?

2 Yo-less only says two lines. How do they tell us that he is a clever sensible boy?

3 We can tell a lot about Johnny from what he says. He has all these qualities:

➤ sensible
➤ sensitive
➤ sentimental
➤ He is a good friend.

Pick out four things in his speech which show these qualities.

4 Johnny's speech is the longest. What effect does this have?

a) It makes him seem like a more important character.
b) It makes him seem more boring than the others.
c) It shows that he feels very strongly about what he is saying.
(Choose the right answer.)

5 What do we learn about Wobbler's character? Explain your answer, using the text.

Setting

The **setting** of a play is important because it is linked to the atmosphere and mood of the play.

Password →

Setting

The **setting** of a story is the place where the action happens. The setting should match the characters and action.

For example, a horror story may be set in a wild, remote place. It would not be as scary set in a supermarket on a busy day!

Most playwrights introduce the setting (and mood) at the opening of the play. Here is the opening of *Johnny and the Dead*.

Scene 1

The cemetery. **Johnny** *walks onto the stage, carrying his schoolbag. He sits on a tombstone and addresses the audience.*

Johnny   I really discovered the cemetery after I started living at Grandad's, after my parents split up. I started taking a short cut through here instead of going home on the bus. My pal Wobbler thinks it's spooky …

Wobbler enters, carrying a schoolbag.

Wobbler   Why do we have to go home this way? I think it's spooky.

Johnny   *[Still talking to the audience]* But I think it's quite … friendly. Peaceful. Once you forget about all the skeletons underground, of course.

1 What is the setting of this story?

2 What is the effect of this setting?

    a) It makes the audience curious.
    b) It confuses the audience.
    c) It makes the audience begin to feel a chill of excitement/fear.

    (Choose the answers you feel are right.)

3 Pick out the words that help to build up the atmosphere:

spooky   schoolbag   underground   tombstone   bus   skeletons

4 Johnny does not think of the cemetery as 'spooky'. How does he hint that there might be more to this place?

The next extract is taken from the play, *Dracula*. Read it carefully, thinking about how the author builds up the atmosphere and mood through the characters and setting.

Jonathan speaks to the audience.

Jonathan   I followed him to the road, and then on to his home – a tall, imposing castle, built on top of a great crag. I didn't really take much of it in, then. I was tired, and still shaken after my ... experience. But I felt better after I'd eaten, and thanked the Count, and said to him that I assumed we'd begin going through the documents the next day.

Dracula turns and speaks to Jonathan.

Dracula   Unfortunately, no. I have to be away during the day on business. I will not be here when you wake. But I shall take the documents with me, and we can go through them together when I return.

Jonathan   When will that be?

Dracula   In the evening.

Jonathan   I see.

Dracula   For tomorrow, my home is yours. There will be food prepared. Spend the day as you wish. I'm sure you will find many things here of interest. But please do confine your wanderings to the house. The chapel, in particular, is in a state of great disrepair, and is not at all safe ...

Dracula turns and walks to the back of the stage. Jonathan speaks to the audience.

Jonathan   I slept fitfully and woke late to a fine, clear day. I found food waiting for me, ate, and then passed the time exploring the many rooms in the castle. But, almost from the moment of my waking, I was increasingly aware of a ... strangeness about the place ... a sense of decay and death ... a rottenness within its very stones.

1 All this scene builds up a mood of unease and fear. Copy and fill in the grid, to help you understand how the author does this. (You may want to note more than one thing in each panel.)

Effect	Word, phrase, line or stage direction that creates the effect
To suggest danger in Dracula's home	Built on an 'imposing' crag.
To suggest approaching danger for Jonathan	
To suggest horror and death	'a sense of decay and death'
To suggest there is something strange about Dracula himself	

2 Use your work to write a mini-essay. Explain how this extract uses the setting and characters to build the atmosphere of danger and horror.

You might want to use some of the following sentence starters:

Jonathan's reaction to ... shows us that ...

Dracula's strange comment that '...

The dangerous chapel further shows us ...

We then see that ...

The feeling of danger builds when ...

In addition to this, ...

The most powerful suggestion that danger approaches is ...

Round-up

With a partner, talk about:
➤ three ways in which we can learn about a character in a play
➤ how a setting can help to create a mood or atmosphere in a play.

Over to you

Now use what you have learnt to write a scene of your own.

Choose your scene. Here are a few ideas:

a football tactics meeting

a plotting session between two criminals

an argument

an awkward talk between parent and child

someone's dying instructions on where to find the gold

a battle scene

 Remember!

Playscripts:
➤ have a special layout
➤ convey characters through speech and action
➤ use stage directions
➤ use setting to build up mood and atmosphere.

Plan

This plan should remind you of how to lay out your playscript.

> *stage direction*
> **Character 1** What he or she says.
> **Character 2** What he or she says.
> **Character 1** What he or she says.
> **Character 2** What he or she says.
> *stage direction*
> **Character 1** What he or she says.
> **Character 2** What he or she says.
> **Character 1** What he or she says.
> etc ...

Now write up your playscript.

When your playscript is finished, try acting it out with your group. Note what works well and what doesn't. You might want to make some changes to your playscript.

In this unit you will:

➤ look at some of the words in poems
➤ look at poetic features and layout
➤ write some poetry, using rhythm, rhyme and imagery.

Get started

By now you will have read lots of different types of poetry, sometimes without realizing it. Don't forget that song lyrics and nursery rhymes are poetry – any beautiful or carefully crafted piece of writing can be poetry.

With a partner, think of three well-known poems, songs or nursery rhymes.

1. Jack and Jill went up the hill
2. All things bright and beautiful
3.

All poetry has one thing in common – it describes something. It could be a story, a person, a place or even just an idea or feeling. This means, that the most important thing in poetry is the *words*.

Not all poetry has to rhyme, and not all poetry has to be set out in verses, or even in straight lines. What is important is that every word is carefully chosen to do a job, and that can be a mixture of what it *means* and how it *sounds*.

An old poem

This poem is about the word 'bookworm' and what it makes the poet think of. Read the poem aloud a few times, so you know where the sentences begin and end.

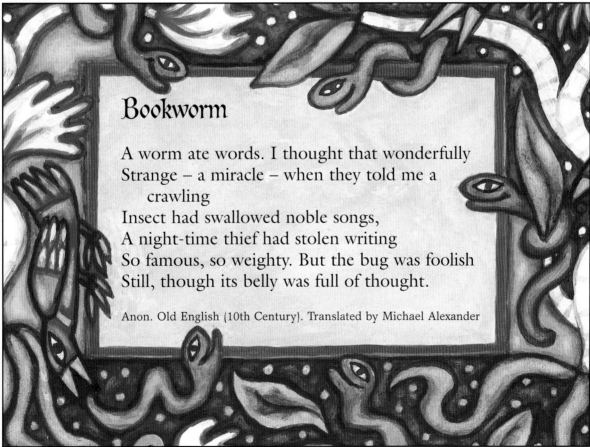

Bookworm

A worm ate words. I thought that wonderfully
Strange – a miracle – when they told me a
    crawling
Insect had swallowed noble songs,
A night-time thief had stolen writing
So famous, so weighty. But the bug was foolish
Still, though its belly was full of thought.

Anon. Old English (10th Century). Translated by Michael Alexander

1   The poem talks about a bookworm as if it is a real bug that eats books. What do we usually mean by the word 'bookworm'?

a) A large worm that looks just like a book.
b) A person that eats books.
c) A person that likes to read books.

(Choose the right answer.)

2   Why do you think the poet uses this word? Choose at least two of the following reasons:

a) To show how strange language can be.
b) To describe the way our imaginations can work.
c) To entertain us.
d) To tell us that insects are stupid.

3   If the 'bookworm' is a person who reads lots of books, is the poet saying that makes him or her clever?
(Hint: look at the last sentence.)

4   Plan a short explanation about what the poet is saying about 'bookworms'. Use some words from the poem to show what you mean.

You may wish to use one of these sentence starters:

The poet is trying to say that bookworms ...

I think the poet means that ...

I don't think the poet is ...

When the poem says, '...' I think it means that ...

The poet uses a **metaphor** to describe the bookworm. Which of the following do you think is that metaphor?

a) 'A night-time thief'
b) 'the bug'
c) 'so weighty'

Metaphors

A **metaphor** is a way of describing something as if it were something else.

For example, if you say 'My brother is a donkey,' you are *not* saying he is brown with four legs, but you *are* saying that he has some of the qualities of a donkey, such as being foolish.

6 Explain why you think that the poet uses this metaphor. (Hint: think about what the poet is saying the insect *does*, and *when*. You may wish to use one of the sentences below to help you.)

The poet uses the metaphor '...' to describe how ...

The word '...' is chosen because it shows that the insect ...

7 Which of the descriptive words below show us that the poet likes the idea of a bookworm?

a) 'the bug was foolish'
b) 'noble songs'
c) 'wonderfully Strange'

8 One line of the poem uses **alliteration**. Which line? Which sounds are repeated?

Password →

Alliteration

Alliteration is when words beginning with the same sound are near each other. Writers use alliteration to emphasize words. Newspaper headlines often use alliteration.

For example:
> *Poorly poodle pees on Prince.*

9 Why do you think the poet has put the word 'crawling' on a line of its own?

a) To make it stand out.
b) To make you say it more slowly when you read it aloud.
c) So that you think of the action of crawling when you read it aloud.
d) It was done by accident.

Choose from these ideas. (Hint: you can choose more than one.)

Traditional rhymes and songs

Read this poem. It is also a popular song.

Twinkle, twinkle, little star

Twinkle, twinkle, little star,
How I wonder what you are.
Up above the world so high,
Like a diamond in the sky.
Twinkle, twinkle, little star,
How I wonder what you are.

1 Who do you think is the audience for this poem? (The people who this poem was written for.) Why do you think the subject of the poem is a 'little star' and not something like a warship or a vampire?

2 Why are all the words in this poem simple, such as 'little', 'sky', 'twinkle', 'world' and 'high'?

    a) Because it makes it easy for little children to understand.
    b) Because it makes it easy for little children to learn.
    c) Because the poet only knew simple words.

    (Choose two of the above answers.)

3 The poet uses repetition (repeats) in this poem. Which words and lines are repeated?

4 Repetition is often used to make something sound important, but it is used for a different reason in this poem. What do you think is the reason? (Hint: think about the audience.)

5 The poet uses a **simile** to describe the star. What is the simile?

Password →

Similes

A **simile** is a way of describing something by comparing it to something else.

For example:
    It's fur was *as* white *as* snow.
    He's *like* Beckham on the pitch.

Note that similes always use the words 'like ...' or 'as ... as ...'

6 Think up four similes to describe a fantastic footballer or another sportsperson. (Hint: think about their skills.)

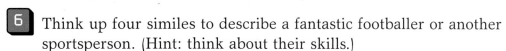

1. He is as fast as lightning.
2. She swims like a fish.
3.
4.

109

7 Count the number of syllables (beats) in each line of the poem, 'Twinkle, twinkle'.

8 Why do you think the poet uses the same number of beats in each line? (Hint: think about remembering poems, and setting them to music.)

Here's another traditional rhyme.

Incy Wincy Spider

Incy Wincy spider climbed up the spout
Down came the rain and washed poor Incy out.
Out came the sunshine and dried up all the rain.
Incy Wincy spider climbed up again.

1 With a partner, think about the main features of this poem. Copy and fill in the grid below.

Features of the poem	Answers/examples
Audience (Who is it for?)	
Subject (Why is it suitable for this audience?)	
Repetition (Where is it used and why?)	
Syllables (How many in each line?)	

2 Many traditional poems use **rhyme**. Pick out the rhyming words in the poem 'Incy Wincy Spider'.

Password →

Rhyme

Words that **rhyme** have the same end sounds.

For example:
m*ay*/cl*ay*
k*ick*/fl*ick*
holid*ay*/run*away*.

3 Have some rhyme races in your group. Everyone has two minutes to think of as many words as they can to rhyme with:

➤ holly
➤ light
➤ eight
➤ shoe.

Writing poetry

Now try writing your own short poem, using 'Twinkle, twinkle' as a model. Follow the steps below:

1 Let's look at the first line.

> *Twinkle, twinkle, little star*
> verb   verb   adjective   noun

Nouns, Verbs and Adjectives

Nouns are people, places, things and emotions, e.g. Prince William, Okehampton, table, sadness.

Verbs are action words, e.g. running, to think, doing, being, to giggle.

Adjectives describe nouns, e.g. pink, foolish, fabulous, complicated, gory.

Write a new version of this first line, but make it the same in three ways:

➤ use the same pattern of words (verb, verb, adjective, noun)
➤ use *seven* syllables in the line
➤ choose a subject suitable for a young child.

For example:

> Giggle, giggle, little boy

or

> Tremble, tremble, sly old fox

Write your own line now.

2 Now look at the second line.

> *How I wonder what you are.*

This line almost asks the subject a question. It has seven syllables. It also rhymes with the line before.

Write your second line now. Try to match it to your first line.

For example:
> Giggle, giggle, little boy
> Do you like your brand new toy?

or
> Tremble, tremble, sly old fox
> Can you smell the hunter's socks?

3 Look back at the third and fourth lines of 'Twinkle, twinkle'.

➤ Both lines again have seven syllables.
➤ Line three describes the subject further.
➤ Line four uses a **simile**.
➤ These two lines also rhyme with each other.

Write the third and fourth lines of your poem.

4 Repeat your first two lines at the end, and you've got your new poem!

5 Sing it to the tune of 'Twinkle, twinkle'. If it doesn't fit the tune, check your syllables!

Round-up

With a partner, list four features that you would include if you were writing a poem. Share your list with another pair, or the rest of the class or group. Discuss which features you think are most important.

Over to you

Write a poem. It could be about a person you know well, an animal, a place, or even a favourite food – anything you like, as long as you can describe it in detail and with some feeling.

> **→ Remember!**
>
> Poems use:
> ➤ metaphors
> ➤ similes
> ➤ repetition
> ➤ alliteration
> ➤ rhyme.

Plan

1. Choose your subject.

2. Decide who your audience is.

3. Jot down ideas for metaphors and/or similes.

4. Think up some pairs of rhyming words, linked to your subject.

5. Write a first draft.

6. Read your draft aloud. Can you improve it by adding:
   ➤ alliteration
   ➤ repetition
   ➤ more interesting adjectives?

7. Write a final draft.

In this unit you will:

➤ look at how writers create their characters, the setting and plot of their stories
➤ write parts of your own story, putting it all together at the end.

Get started

A good story can be about anything, but it has to have three key things to make it work:

Characters

They don't have to be people. There can be one or more. The story is about what happens to the characters.

Settings

Every story has to be set somewhere.
The setting can be anywhere, e.g. another planet, virtual reality, or inside someone's head!

Plot

The plot is the action of the story.
It tells us what happens.

1 With a partner, think of a story that you both know. (It could be a film, TV programme or book.) Jot down:

> ➤ the name of one or two characters
> ➤ the setting (there may be lots, but choose the main one)
> ➤ an outline of the plot (one or two sentences only).

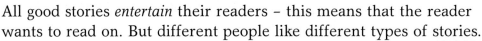

All good stories *entertain* their readers – this means that the reader wants to read on. But different people like different types of stories. Your gran might enjoy a love story set in the year 1674, whereas you may prefer a crime thriller set in space. Luckily, different writers like to write different types of stories, so there is a wide range of **genres** to choose from.

Password →

Genres

A **genre** is a type. Stories can be sorted into lots of different genres, e.g. adventure, crime, science fiction, historical, fantasy, comedy, horror, romance.

Some stories are a mix of genre, e.g. historical romance.

2 List three of your favourite genres. Then put examples of stories beside them. (They can be films, TV programmes or books.)

> science fiction – Stargate, Star Trek
> fantasy – Harry Potter
> comedy

Character

A character in a story can be any sort of person or being:

young   **old**   *female*   *animal*   **male**   **machine**

With a partner, think of six characters (from stories) who each match one of the descriptions above.

A character has to be believable, so it is important that the writer describes them well. This can be done in different ways:

You can describe *what they look like*, e.g. 'He always wore Armani suits with dark glasses – no-one had ever seen his eyes.'

You can describe them by *something they do*, e.g. 'Mrs Lowe never forgot the birds in the garden, taking her scraps to the bird-table every lunchtime, rain or shine.'

What they say can reveal a lot about them, e.g. 'I don't think we can allow your sort of person into this establishment, dear me, no,' she said.

You can describe *their personality*, e.g. 'Amy was always ready with a cheeky comment.'

What others say about them can reveal what they are like, e.g. 'The soldiers of the Devonshire Regiment would never hear a word against Sergeant Guscott, saying he was a tyrant with a heart of gold.'

Read this extract from a story. It describes the villain of the book, Count Olaf.

1 Count Olaf was neither interesting nor kind; he was demanding, short-tempered, and
   bad-smelling. The only good thing to be said for Count Olaf is that he wasn't around
3 very often. When the children woke up and chose their clothing out of the refrigerator
   box, they would walk into the kitchen and find a list of instructions left for them by
5 Count Olaf, who would often not appear till night time. Most of the day he spent out
   of the house, or up in the high tower, where the children were forbidden to go. The
7 instructions he left for them were usually difficult chores, such as repainting the back
   porch or repairing the windows, and instead of a signature Count Olaf would draw an
9 eye at the bottom of the note.

From *A Series of Unfortunate Events* by Lemony Snicket

1 In the *first* sentence, the writer tells us about Count Olaf by:

a) what others say about him
b) describing his personality
c) showing us what he does.
(Choose the right answer.)

2 We are told that Count Olaf is 'bad-smelling.' What other qualities does that suggest he may have? Pick *four* of the following:

horrible
kind
lazy
hard-working
mean
grumpy
unpleasant
sporty
ill
evil
charitable
clean

3 What is 'the only good thing' to be said for Count Olaf, and what does it tell us about him?
Use the sentence below to help you write your answer.

'We learn that Count Olaf is ... because the only good thing about him is ...'

4 We learn more about Count Olaf from something he does. Look at lines 4 to 7 to find out what that is. Explain what it tells us about him.

5 In the last line, the writer gives us an **idiosyncratic detail** about Count Olaf. What is it?

Idiosyncratic detail

Idiosyncratic detail is a little bit of information that does not fit in with the usual picture. When a writer gives idiosyncratic detail about a character it makes them seem a bit different and makes us curious. It often gives a clue about their personality.

For example:
A tough bodybuilder with a tiny kitten tattooed on his arm.
A head teacher who always has his teddy in his briefcase.

6 What do you think the idiosyncratic detail suggests about Count Olaf's character?

a) He is always somehow watching the children.
b) He has really bad eyesight.
c) He runs a secret spy organization.
d) He goes to art classes.
(Choose at least one answer.)

7 The last clue we get about Count Olaf is his *title*. What is it about his title that makes him seem evil?
(Hint: what other famous villain is a Count?)

Round-up

With a partner, list four ways that writers portray characters. Talk about whether one way is more powerful than another.

Over to you

Now your task is to create a character of your own.

> → **Remember!**
>
> Tell the reader about your character by
> ➤ how they look
> ➤ what they do
> ➤ what they say
> ➤ what other characters say about them
> ➤ idiosyncratic detail.

Plan

Use this mind-map to help you plan your character:

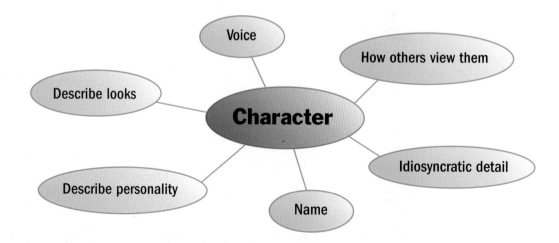

1 You might wish to follow these steps to create your character.

Will your character be ...	Your answer
human or otherwise?	
male or female?	
hero or villain?	
what occupation? (wizard, binman, spy?)	
old or young?	
attractive or unattractive?	
popular or unpopular?	

2 Think about what your character looks like. Draw a simple sketch with labels.
For example:

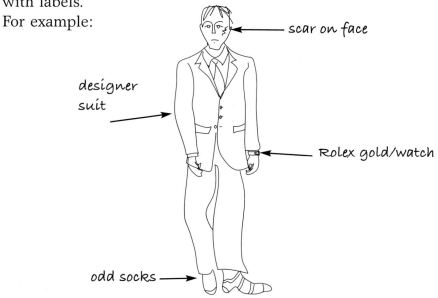

scar on face

designer suit

Rolex gold/watch

odd socks

3 Now think about what those looks say about the personality and history of your character. For example, the character above might be a rich gangster, ruthless, violent and colour-blind!

4 Decide how your character will speak. Will they tend to be **formal** or **informal**? Will they have an accent?

Password →

Formal/Informal

Formal speaking and writing is used in important, public or business situations, e.g. in an interview, a meeting with the head teacher, an essay, a letter to a bank manager.

Informal speaking and writing is used in private, casual situations, e.g. with friends, on postcards, text messages.

5 Now give your character a name. Choose a name that gives the reader a clue about their personality. For example, Loretta McSwine-Daggers or Cecil Slitheringby!

Keep your work for use at the end of the unit.

Setting

A good setting gives a story atmosphere and mood.

Password →

Setting

The **setting** of a story is the place where the action happens. The setting should match the characters and action.

For example, a horror story may be set in a strange, ancient building in a remote area.

Suggest suitable settings for:

➤ a romantic short story
➤ a tale of survival and adventure
➤ a story about a soldier fighting a battle.

Read this description of a setting. The heroine, Tiffany, has just arrived in the very strange land of an evil Queen. She has come to rescue her brother.

No sun in the sky. Even on the dullest days, you could generally see where the sun was, but not here. And there was something else that was strange, something she couldn't quite give a name to. This didn't feel like a real place. She didn't know why she felt that, but something was wrong with the horizon. It looked close enough to touch, which was silly … The trees here were different. She had a strong feeling that they were blobs, and were growing the roots and twigs and other details as she got closer, as if they were thinking, 'Quick, someone's coming! Look real!'

It was like being in a painting where the artist hadn't bothered much with the things in the distance, but had quickly rushed a bit of realness anywhere you were looking.

The air was cold and dead, like the air in old cellars.

The light grew dimmer as they reached the forest. In between the trees it became blue and eerie.

No birds, she thought.

From *The Wee Free Men* by Terry Pratchett

1. Tiffany notices there is no sun. Why does she say that is odd?

2. She also notices there are no birds. Why would that make anybody nervous?

3. There are two similes which help to describe the place. What are they? (Hint: similes use the words 'as … as,' or 'like …')

4. Re-read the paragraph about the trees. Do you think they are alarming because:

   a) trees aren't meant to think
   b) trees are supposed to grow over years, not minutes
   c) it seems like someone unseen is in charge of where she is
   d) the twig might reach out and grab her
   (Choose any answers you feel are right.)

5 In this description, the author has appealed to some of the reader's senses. This makes a setting feel more real, because you can imagine what it would be like to be there. Copy and complete the grid below.

Sense	Examples
Sight	Trees that change, 'and were growing the roots and twigs and other details as she got closer.' 'The light grew dimmer'
Sound	
Smell/taste	
Touch	

Round-up

With a partner, match these settings to suitable stories. Be prepared to explain your choices.

Settings	Stories
a beautiful tropical island	murder mystery
a colony on Mars	science fiction
a desolate, wild mountain range	romance
a haunted castle	adventure
a country house full of weekend guests	horror

Over to you

Now create your own setting. Think of a suitable place for the character you created in the last section.

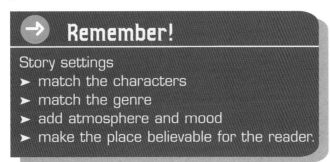

→ **Remember!**

Story settings
➤ match the characters
➤ match the genre
➤ add atmosphere and mood
➤ make the place believable for the reader.

Plan

You might find it useful to draw up a mind-map to jot down your ideas:

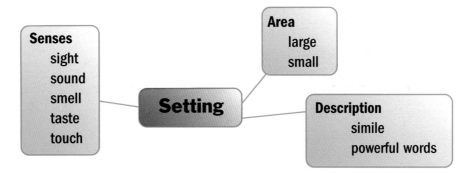

Use the steps below to help you describe your setting.

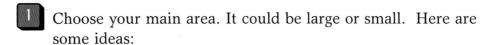

1 Choose your main area. It could be large or small. Here are some ideas:

Large area	Small area
A city – London? New York?	A classroom
A holiday resort – Barcelona? Blackpool?	A dusty basement
An Olympic stadium	A tent
A desert	An attic room
An old theatre	An office at the top of a tower block
A huge Scottish castle	A penthouse suite in a hotel
Wild moorland	A recording studio
	A royal bedroom

2 Now think about the detail of your setting. What does it feel like to be there? Use the five senses to guide you.

sight -
sound -
smell -
taste -
touch -

3 Write a first draft to describe your setting.
➤ Try to use powerful, interesting words.
➤ Include a simile.

Keep your work for use later on in the unit.

Plot

The plot of the story is what happens – the action. The plot usually has a basic **story structure**.

Password →

Story structure

A **story structure** usually follows a pattern which has four parts:

The opening – which grabs the reader's attention so they want to know more
The complication – where the main problem/task is revealed
The crisis – where the problem/task comes to a head, often dramatically
The resolution – where the problem is solved, and the ending can be reached.

Note that this pattern can be repeated many times in a story.

Read this extract from *Robinson Crusoe*, by Daniel Defoe. The hero has just been shipwrecked on a desert island, and none of his companions have survived.

I began to look round me to see what kind of place I was in, and what was next to be done, and I soon found my comforts abate, and that in a word I had a dreadful deliverance: For I was wet, had no clothes to shift me, nor anything either to eat or drink to comfort me, neither did I see any prospect before me, but that of perishing with hunger, or being devour'd by wild beasts; and that which was particularly afflicting to me, was, that I had no weapon either to hunt and kill any creature for my sustenance, or to defend my self against any other creature that might desire to kill me for theirs: In a word, I had nothing about me but a knife, a tobacco-pipe, and a little tobacco in a box, this was all my provision, and this threw me into terrible agonies of mind, that for a while I ran about like a mad-man; night coming upon me, I began with a heavy heart to consider what would be my lot if there were any ravenous beasts in that country, seeing at night they always come abroad for their prey.

Glossary

abate – stop
deliverance – rescue
devour'd – eaten
prospect – future
provision – supplies
ravenous – starving
 hungry
shift – dress
sustenance – food

1 What part of the story structure do you think this episode is?

a) the opening
b) the complication
c) the crisis
d) the resolution

2 Robinson Crusoe says he has had a 'dreadful deliverance'. What do you think he means by that?

3 Crusoe has five immediate problems. What are they?

4 How do we know that Robinson is basically sensible?

a) He is worried about having no food.
b) He runs about like a 'mad-man'.
c) He counts up his supplies.
d) He is afraid of hungry beasts in the night.
(Choose all the answers that you think are correct.)

5 What clues are we given for what might be coming up in the story?

Round-up

With a partner, think of a well-known story. Divide it up into the four main sections of story structure.

Over to you

Now create a plot of your own, for your character and setting from the last sections.

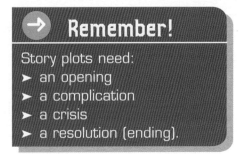

→ **Remember!**

Story plots need:
➤ an opening
➤ a complication
➤ a crisis
➤ a resolution (ending).

Plan

Use a mind-map to jot down your first ideas about the action and plot of your story.

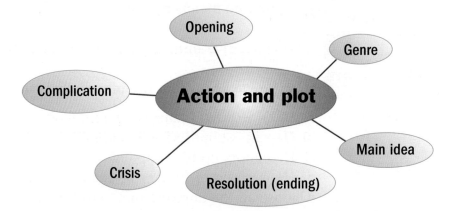

Follow the steps below to draft the structure of your story.

First, decide on the **genre** of your story.

Then, decide on your main idea. It must involve solving a problem or a challenge, e.g. a robbery, an argument, winning a match, dealing with bullies, etc.

Use a plot plan, like the one below, to help you decide on your story structure.

Story structure	Notes
The opening ➤ introduce the main character ➤ describe the scene or situation	
The complication ➤ the character has to face his or her challenge/problem ➤ describe the action ➤ show the character's emotions	
The crisis ➤ action should be dramatic, dangerous, fast-paced ➤ show the character's emotions	
The resolution (ending) ➤ clear up whatever situation has been the subject of the story ➤ include a comment or action from the main character ➤ remember that the best stories often surprise the reader at the end!	

Tips

The opening and ending of your story is very important. Here are some 'DO's and 'DON'T's:

Openings:

Do introduce your character.
Do make the reader curious.
Do start the action.

Don't start 'Once upon a time'.
Don't bore the reader with too much information.
Don't confuse the reader with too many characters.

Endings:

Do leave the reader satisfied and 'in the know'.
Do try to include a twist to entertain the reader.
Do include a comment from the main character.

Don't end with the story as a dream or alien abduction.
Don't make the ending too obvious.
Don't introduce a new character at the end.

Writing your story in full

You have worked on many different parts of your story. Now try putting it all together.

Follow the steps below.

→ Remember!

Stories need:
➤ at least one character
➤ a setting
➤ a plot.

1. Write a first draft.

2. Share it with a partner and ask for their comments.

3. Re-read and then edit your draft to improve it.

4. Proofread your work, checking spelling, punctuation and paragraphing.

5. Display your finished story.

In this unit you will:

➤ look at some reviews and reading journals
➤ write a review of a film or book of your choice
➤ write an entry for a reading journal.

The Matrix

That was the best film I've ever seen...

Get started

When was the last time you told someone about a film or TV programme that you saw or gave your **opinion** about a book that you read? Whenever you do this, you are giving a 'review'. Some people are paid to write reviews, and these are what you read in newspapers and magazines. Reviews can be about films, plays, books, CDs, DVDs – in fact anything that people are interested in seeing, listening to, reading or buying.

The word 'review' is made up of the prefix 're-' which means 'to do something again', and the verb 'view'. So it literally means 'to look at something again'.

Password →

Opinion

An **opinion** is someone's view, e.g. about whether a book is exciting or boring, or whether a computer game is worth buying. (Compare this with **facts**, which can be proven.)

Choose a film you have seen recently. Tell a partner a bit about the film (without giving away the whole story), giving them some **facts**. Then explain why you liked or disliked it. Ask each other questions to clarify your opinions. Then, tell the rest of the class about your chosen film. You have just given a review!

Password →

Facts

Facts are something that can be proved to be true.

For example:
➤ the author of a book
➤ the actors in a film
➤ the type of music on a CD.

Film review

Read the review of the film *Pirates of the Caribbean* on page 133.

PIRATES of the CARIBBEAN
THE CURSE OF THE BLACK PEARL

On a foggy sea a boat suddenly happens upon the blazing wreck of a mighty ship. There is only one survivor – a boy on a makeshift raft. Around his neck is a gold medallion. The girl who cares for him takes the trinket, and as she does so, sees a ghostly ship, its sails in tatters, ploughing through the waves back into the fog.

Ten years later the girl is revealed as the governor's daughter and the boy who was rescued is now a blacksmith. Before you can shout 'Shiver me timbers' they are both involved in a battle with Captain Barbarossa and the crew of the *Black Pearl*, a legendary pirate ship.

So begins this hugely entertaining tale with striking visuals, loud battle sequences, swordfights and the grungiest pirates ever seen. While it is 30 minutes too long and loses pace after the first hour, this is nevertheless fabulous stuff. It has everything – valiant heroes, damsels in distress, hissable baddies and great stunts. For sheer fun it cannot be beaten!

Adapted from the *Yorkshire Post* 'The Guide', 8 August 2003

---

1 The purpose of this text is to:

➤ warn parents the film is too violent for children
➤ inform people about what happens in the film
➤ give an opinion about whether the film is worth going to see.
(Choose the correct answer.)

2 Who do you think is the **audience** for this review? Why?

Password →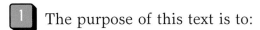

Audience

The **audience** is the people who read the text.

3 The article is in three paragraphs. What information does each paragraph give you? Use the sentence starters below to help you.

The first paragraph tells the reader ...

In the second paragraph, the writer explains ...

The third paragraph gives a general ...

4 Why does the writer not say what happens at the end of the film?

5 The writer uses **facts** and **opinions** in his review. Pick out two more facts and two more opinions and add them to the grid below.

Facts	Opinions
There is a battle with Captain Barbarossa	The film is 30 minutes too long

6 What **verb tense** does the writer use? Pick out five verbs from the review. Write each verb in another sentence using the same tense.

Password →

Verb tense

Verbs can be written in the **past**, **present** or **future tense**.

For example:
    The pirates *attacked* the ship. (past tense)
    The pirates *attack* the ship. (present tense)
    The pirates *will attack* the ship. (future tense)

7 The writer uses **adjectives** to describe different parts of the film. List five phrases that use adjectives.

Password →

Adjectives

An **adjective** is a describing word that gives more information about something.

For example:
    A *violent* battle
    A *huge* burger.

Book review

Read this review of *Stone Cold* by Robert Swindells. It is taken from a book review website, www.mrsmad.co.uk.

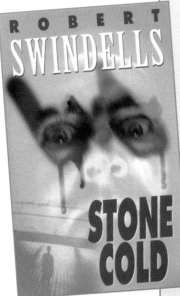

What's it about?

A homeless boy on the streets of London faces a desperate fight for life when his friends start to disappear.

What happens?

Link wasn't born homeless, after his parents split up he couldn't bear living in the same house as his mother's new boyfriend. But after he leaves he has a run of bad luck and no choice but to end up on the streets of London. Life is hard, cold and unfriendly, until he meets Ginger. His new friend shows Link how to survive, where to go for shelter and where the best begging places are. Then Ginger disappears and Link makes a new friend, Gail. He stops worrying about everything else, but other kids are still vanishing. Will it be Link's turn next?

Is it easy to read?

Written in two parts, with a change in print type to help the reader recognise who is talking. Easy to read, but requires some maturity to understand the contents. Recommended reading for all young readers who are becoming aware of the world around them.

Anything else?

A hauntingly tragic story. This is incredibly well written, Swindells writes about issues which are happening every day all around us. The easy slide of Link's into homelessness is so simple it is shocking. There is an urgency in this story and a world exposed as uncaring about the unwanted youths on our streets.

1 How does the writer divide up the text?

2 Why do you think questions make good sub-headings?

3 Look at the list of sub-headings on the left, below. Link them to the correct description of paragraphs on the right.

Sub-headings

What's it about?

What happens?

Is it easy to read?

Anything else?

Description of paragraphs

Comments about how the story is written and its audience

A brief outline of the story

More detail about the story, including the names of some characters

Comments about how realistic the story is

Comparing reviews

1 Use the grid to compare the film review with the book review.

	Pirates of the Caribbean	Stone Cold
Type of Review	Film	Book
How does the review begin?		
How much story detail is given?		
What are the good features?		
What are the bad features?		
Which verb tense is used?		
What adjectives are used?		
What comments are made about the audience?		

2 Do the reviews share many of the same features?

Over to you

Now try writing a review of your own about a film or a book. You might want to work with a partner.

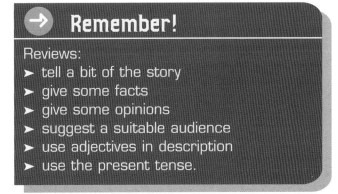

→ **Remember!**

Reviews:
- ➤ tell a bit of the story
- ➤ give some facts
- ➤ give some opinions
- ➤ suggest a suitable audience
- ➤ use adjectives in description
- ➤ use the present tense.

Plan

Follow these steps to plan your review:

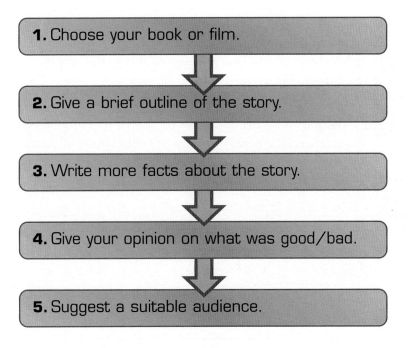

1. Choose your book or film.

2. Give a brief outline of the story.

3. Write more facts about the story.

4. Give your opinion on what was good/bad.

5. Suggest a suitable audience.

Now write your review in full.

Reading Journals

A reading journal is a sort of diary. It is a record of your thoughts about a book as you read it. A reading journal is more personal than a review, because the **audience** is usually only the writer (and maybe a teacher).

Here are some extracts from a reading journal, written by a student. He is writing about the book *Artemis Fowl* by Eoin Colfer. The writing has been annotated (explained with extra notes) to help you see the sort of things that you might want to put in a reading journal.

Uses a quote from the 'blurb' to show what interests him

Honest comments about the opening pages and what he's done to help himself

Picks out things that he finds funny

Shows sympathy for character

I have picked 'Artemis Fowl' to read. It looks interesting because on the back it says he is a 'brilliant criminal mastermind' and I like crime and adventure stories, but he's only 12 – like me. It says he kidnaps a fairy. I'm not really into fairy stories any more but these fairies are armed and dangerous so they're not like fairy godmothers.

The start is quite hard. There are some words I had to look up, like 'pessimism'. It means to look on the bad side of things. I like Artemis though. He has a giant butler called Butler, which is funny. The butler is a martial arts expert so I hope later on he does some fighting. Artemis sounds like a genius. He knows about computers and spots things about people and knows what drugs to give to make you forget things.

I feel sorry for Artemis now. His mum is ill with some sort of mental illness because his dad has disappeared. He has to live on his own with Butler most of the time. I wouldn't want that sort of life even if I was a millionaire and a genius. I don't know how I'd cope without my family. I'd like to ask him what it's like to have to rely on just servants and to have to work things out for yourself without any parents to advise you.

Explains what he likes to read

Chooses some details about the character to show why he sounds like a genius.

Comments about the situation the character faces

Has questions he'd like to ask characters

1 What reasons does the student give for picking the book *Artemis Fowl*?

2 What sort of stories does the student say he is *not* into anymore?

a) crime stories
b) adventure stories
c) fairy stories.
(Choose the correct answer.)

3 List three **facts** about Artemis that the student mentions.

4 How does the student feel about the characters?

5 How do we know that the student is thinking about what might happen later in the book?

6 How is this text divided up?

7 Why do you think it is divided up like this? (Think about what each section focuses on.)

8 In a reading journal, which of the following might you include?:

a) a description of the character or the setting
b) your ideas about how the story will end
c) comments about other things you've read that have similar events or ideas
e) what you like and dislike about the story

9 Which **verb tense** is used most in this reading journal extract?

10 Do you think the student is enjoying this book? Complete the sentences below to write your answer.

I think the student ... because he says ...

He also comments about ... which seems to suggest ...

Over to you

Write an entry for a reading journal. Choose a book you are reading in class or at home.

> **Remember!**
>
> Reading journals:
> ➤ are written at different stages of reading
> ➤ record personal feelings and ideas about a book
> ➤ comment on characters and plot
> ➤ can suggest what happens next
> ➤ can record new words
> ➤ are written mainly in the present tense.

Plan

Use a plan to help you organize your reading journal entry.

Title and author of book

↓

Who the main characters are. What you think about them

First impressions of opening section

↓

Problems or challenges that the characters face. How you think they might resolve them

How the writer makes the events interesting/funny/scary/realistic

↓

Whether other people might enjoy this book

↓

Where and when the story takes place. What you think of the author's setting

Round-up

Reviews and reading journals are similar in some ways, but different in others. With a partner, list the similarities and differences between reviews and reading journals. (Use the Remember! panels to help you.)

Talk about which sort of writing you have enjoyed most.

Quiz

Here is a quiz that you can do alone, with a partner, in a group, or with the whole class.

In the grid below there is a summary of the key features of each text type. Test what you know:

1 Cover up the Features column.

2 Look at the name of the Text type and the cartoon.

3 Name some of the key features of that text type.

4 Check your answer by looking at the Features column.

5 For an extra challenge, try to think of another possible feature of each text type.

(Note that not all texts of one type contain all the listed features. These are a general guide only.)

Text type	Features
Information texts 	Information texts use: ➤ the present tense ➤ the third person ➤ clear layout (sub-headings, topic sentences, illustration) ➤ they are written for a particular audience.
Recounts  How will I recount this to my friends?	Recounts use: ➤ the past tense ➤ chronological order ➤ time connectives ➤ complex sentences.
Explanations  SO, DOC, WILL YOU EXPLAIN WHAT TREATMENT I'LL NEED?	Explanations use: ➤ the present tense ➤ the third person ➤ sequence (to link points clearly) ➤ technical language.
Instructions 	Instructions use: ➤ imperative verbs ➤ sequence (to show the right order) ➤ connectives.

Text type	Features
Persuasive texts 	Persuasive texts use: ➤ repetition ➤ exaggeration ➤ rhetorical questions ➤ imperatives.
Discursive texts 	Discursive texts need: ➤ an introduction to the topic ➤ two or more points of view ➤ facts and opinions ➤ a conclusion that includes the writer's opinion.
Advice texts 	Advice texts: ➤ use a mix of instruction, persuasion, explanation and information ➤ are written for a particular audience ➤ often use the second person ('you') ➤ use a tone suited to the topic and audience.
Description 	Descriptions use: ➤ noun phrases ➤ similes ➤ clues for the reader to infer and deduce ➤ a variety of sentence types.

Text type	Features
Plays 	Playscripts: ➤ have a special layout ➤ convey characters through speech and action ➤ use stage directions ➤ use setting to build up mood and atmosphere.
Poetry 	Poems use: ➤ metaphors ➤ alliteration ➤ similes ➤ rhyme. ➤ repetition
Stories 	Stories need: ➤ at least one character ➤ a setting ➤ a plot.
Reviews and reading journals 	Reviews: ➤ tell a bit of the story ➤ give facts and opinions ➤ suggest a suitable audience ➤ use adjectives in description ➤ use the present tense. Reading journals: ➤ are written at different stages of reading ➤ record personal feelings and ideas about a book ➤ comment on characters and plot ➤ can suggest what happens next ➤ can record new words ➤ are written mainly in the present tense.